Off to COLLEGE:
Now What?

A Practical Guide to Surviving and
Succeeding Your First Year in College

By
Jessica Linnell

Off To College: Now What? A Practical Guide To Surviving and Succeeding Your First In College

Copyright © 2009 Atlantic Publishing Group, Inc.
1405 SW 6th Avenue • Ocala, Florida 34471 • Phone 800-814-1132 • Fax 352-622-1875
Web site: www.atlantic-pub.com • E-mail: sales@atlantic-pub.com
SAN Number: 268-1250

ISBN-13: 978-1-60138-314-3   ISBN-10: 1-60138-314-2

Library of Congress Cataloging-in-Publication Data

Linnell, Jessica, 1979-
  Off to college : now what? a practical guide to surviving and succeeding your first year of college / by Jessica Linnell.
      p. cm.
  Includes bibliographical references and index.
  ISBN-13: 978-1-60138-314-3 (alk. paper)
  ISBN-10: 1-60138-314-2 (alk. paper)
  1. College freshmen--United States--Conduct of life. I. Title.

  LA229.L438 2009
  378.1'98--dc22
                      2008035308

Printed in the United States

Printed on Recycled Paper

COVER DESIGN: Vickie Taylor • vtaylor@atlantic-pub.com
PROJECT MANAGER: Melissa Peterson • mpeterson@atlantic-pub.com
INTERIOR DESIGN: Shannon Preston

We recently lost our beloved pet "Bear," who was not only our best and dearest friend but also the "Vice President of Sunshine" here at Atlantic Publishing. He did not receive a salary but worked tirelessly 24 hours a day to please his parents. Bear was a rescue dog that turned around and showered myself, my wife Sherri, his grandparents Jean, Bob and Nancy and every person and animal he met (maybe not rabbits) with friendship and love. He made a lot of people smile every day.

We wanted you to know that a portion of the profits of this book will be donated to The Humane Society of the United States.

— *Douglas & Sherri Brown*

THE HUMANE SOCIETY
OF THE UNITED STATES ©

The human-animal bond is as old as human history. We cherish our animal companions for their unconditional affection and acceptance. We feel a thrill when we glimpse wild creatures in their natural habitat or in our own backyard.

Unfortunately, the human-animal bond has at times been weakened. Humans have exploited some animal species to the point of extinction.

The Humane Society of the United States makes a difference in the lives of animals here at home and worldwide. The HSUS is dedicated to creating a world where our relationship with animals is guided by compassion. We seek a truly humane society in which animals are respected for their intrinsic value, and where the human-animal bond is strong.

Want to help animals? We have plenty of suggestions. Adopt a pet from a local shelter, join The Humane Society and be a part of our work to help companion animals and wildlife. You will be funding our educational, legislative, investigative and outreach projects in the U.S. and across the globe.

Or perhaps you'd like to make a memorial donation in honor of a pet, friend or relative? You can through our Kindred Spirits program. And if you'd like to contribute in a more structured way, our Planned Giving Office has suggestions about estate planning, annuities, and even gifts of stock that avoid capital gains taxes.

Maybe you have land that you would like to preserve as a lasting habitat for wildlife. Our Wildlife Land Trust can help you. Perhaps the land you want to share is a backyard—that's enough. Our Urban Wildlife Sanctuary Program will show you how to create a habitat for your wild neighbors.

So you see, it's easy to help animals. And The HSUS is here to help.

The Humane Society of the United States
2100 L Street NW
Washington, DC 20037
202-452-1100
www.hsus.org

Acknowledgements

I would like to thank my family and friends who have believed in me throughout my life and writing career. A special thanks to all the experts who submitted advice to students and shared their experiences with readers. I would also like to make a special dedication to Robert Linnell, my late grandfather. He was an inspiration to me and always encouraged me to shoot for my goals, stand up for what I believe, and work hard in all I do.

Table Of Contents

Chapter 8: Dorm Life 123

Chapter 9: Am I Rooming with an Ax Murderer? 129

Chapter 12: Risky Business: Sex 171

Chapter 13: Packing It On: Healthy Advice 181

Chapter 14: Sneezes, Sniffles, and Coughs 195

Chapter 18: The Balancing Act: Work and College............ 235

Chapter 19: Three Years to Go.......... 243

Foreword

I closed the door to North Hall room 329 and turned around. As I looked past the new computer on the desk and the waist-high refrigerator sitting next to the extra-long twin bed, I could see Ben Hill Griffin Stadium staring back at me. After a few moments, I saw two people walk across the street toward the parking lot. They stopped, turned, looked for my window, and waved. I waved back. Mom and Dad were going home…without me.

I was excited, nervous, anxious, and motivated. Name the emotion; I was feeling it that August afternoon at the University of Florida. I was now a Florida Gator, and there was no turning back. This was not a high school with 900 students where every teacher knew my name. This was a campus of 45,000 people where you were lucky to find a parking spot. My roommate was a friend from high school and had not arrived yet. I had no idea what to do next except unpack and hook up my computer. Unpacking went well, but getting the Internet to work was a different story. While struggling to figure out what an Ethernet cord was (who knew it did not come with the computer), I took a break and went to eat dinner at the dining hall. Luckily, another friend from high school who lived in the residence hall next to mine had a meal plan too. I explained my computer issues to him while we ate our first college meal.

There is more to the freshman experience than just picking out sheets and towels and searching for your new roommate on Facebook. Going to college is a life-altering experience. Author Jessica Linnell's *Off to College: Now What? A Practical Guide to Surviving and Succeeding Your First Year of College* will empower you to prepare for college, make decisions after you arrive, and have a successful first year.

I was given a book similar to this one before going to college. It was an excellent resource to me and other freshmen that I got to know on my floor. It gave good insights and suggestions on how to succeed as a freshman, and I found myself pulling it out at different times throughout my first semester. Similarly, this book will provide you with the same useful information in an easy-to-read format that includes tips from fellow students and college administrators.

Although college is, in large part, an academic experience, there are so many other things to consider. Have you thought about how to get involved on campus? Do you know what to do if you do not get along with your roommate? Have you created a monthly budget? What will it be like the first time you visit home? These questions and many more will be answered in Linnell's book, which will prepare you for what to expect. It is guaranteed to guide you through your first year of college.

After finishing my first year in college, I looked up at the window to North Hall room 329 before I pulled away. I was going home for the summer. Nine months had passed, but it seemed like I had just moved in. I finally got the Internet working, got used to wearing shower shoes, realized that attending a 7:30 a.m. class was challenging, and learned not to drive my car during the middle of a weekday if I wanted a parking spot when I returned. I smiled as I pulled away because I had done what one had said I could not.

I survived, and so can you!

Kelly R. Doel
Area Coordinator
University of Central Florida
kdoel@mail.ucf.edu

Kelly Doel is an Area Coordinator with the Department of Housing and Residence Life at the University of Central Florida. She began her career at Florida Atlantic University after attending the University of Florida where she earned a bachelor's degree in English (2003) and a master's in Secondary English Education (2004). While attending the University of Florida, Doel worked as a Resident Assistant and Graduate Hall Director for the Department of Housing and Residence Education and was inducted into the James C. Grimm Chapter of the National Residence Hall Honorary in 2001. She was also the personal assistant to professor and author James Haskins.

Doel is involved with the Association of College and University Housing Officers International and the National Association of Student Personnel Administrators. She has experience with on- and off-campus housing communities and has worked with freshmen, upperclassmen, graduate students, and athletes. In addition, she has instructed a community-service-based leadership course for sophomore students at UCF and has advised student groups for five years.

Doel was also a contributor to the book "The College Roommate from Hell: Skills and Strategies for Surviving College With a Problem Roommate."

Preface

Why This Book Was Written and How It Relates to Today's Environment

If you are reading this book, it is likely that you are going to college or at least considering a college path. You might be getting nervous or anxious to leave home. You are facing the decision of whether to attend college close to home or far away. You might have already decided on what college you will be attending. At this point, whether you have already graduated from high school or are rounding out your senior year, you are starting to focus on the college life.

Going to college can be an exciting and scary experience. This book will help you embrace all that college has to offer. It will help you put aside some fears you may have of the unknown college experience. After reading this book, you will be armed with the knowledge and understanding you need to successfully navigate through your freshman year of college.

Looking Back and Aiming Forward

Congratulations on your high school graduation. You should be proud of yourself. You may also know what college you will be attending next fall. If all goes well, that school was one of your top picks if not your first choice. Take a minute to reflect on your accomplishment, pat yourself on the back, and do not forget all the hard work that got you where you are today. All right, enough of that. You now need to prepare for a four-year college experience.

Luckily, you are not in this alone. You have a support system consisting of family, friends, high school counselors, college advisors, and now this book. Some of you may be lucky enough to have older siblings or friends who have already gone to college to give you a firsthand account of what to expect — and what not to expect. If not, do not fret. This book will guide you.

How This Book Will Help You

The goal of this book is to prepare you for the challenges and pitfalls you might encounter in your freshman year. Your college experience should be fulfilling and rewarding. You should be looking forward to your experience and be prepared for it.

This book was compiled using the latest research in surviving college, interviews with numerous professionals, and accounts of recent freshmen to offer the most up-to-date and comprehensive guide to surviving your freshman year. As the U.S. Census Bureau reports, more than 500,000 students begin their freshman year of college each year, and so this book is needed. Especially considering that of those 500,000 entering freshmen, 150,000 will not make it to their sophomore year. That is a 30 percent dropout rate.

Although the reasons college freshmen drop out vary from too much partying to trouble with finances to missing home, with a little preparation and the helpful tips in this book, you can be among the students who make it through to graduation. Even though this book focuses on the freshman year of college, the advice and tips you will learn can help you navigate through your entire college experience so that in four years you will be receiving another diploma — this time, your college diploma.

Introduction

How the Book Is Organized and What Readers Can Expect to Learn

A successful freshman year — and college experience, for that matter — comes from being prepared. College will be full of unexpected twists and turns. You will be faced with new challenges and enjoy unimaginable successes. Preparing for this, before you are bombarded with new situations, new issues, and new joys, will help you navigate through your first year of college. That is not to say you will not face bumps along the path or that you will never fall short of the expectations you have for yourself or that others have for you. But being prepared and learning the importance of balancing your time and maintaining an organized schedule will help you pick yourself up from any hiccups along the way.

This book is a comprehensive guide to surviving your first year of school. It will focus on the four essential cornerstones of a successful college career. Those cornerstones — study, friends, health, and involvement — paired with other major concerns, including transitioning from high school to college, finances, and graduation, are all covered in this book. Advice from recent and successful college freshmen, college advisors, professors, and others will help guide you through this transition.

This book is divided into seven sections that cover the basic survival tools for college freshmen today: *Transitioning from High School to College, Study, Friends, Health, Involvement, Finances,* and *Graduation.* Within these sections, the individual chapters cover specific areas and offer helpful tips. You will read about study tips, time management skills, sound financial guidelines, and advice on dating and making friends. Dorm decorating, packing lists, and learning how to deal with roommate turmoil will also be discussed.

Although reading this book from cover to cover is most likely the best method, you may choose to skip around to read the topics of most importance to you. Yet, it is best to begin reading with the first section, *Transitioning from High School to College.* Whether you will be leaving home and living in a dorm room or staying at home and attending a local school, this section will help you learn what will and will not change. It will help you deal with the transition of living with strict rules to living with hardly any. It will also help you realize the transition your family and friends will face as you move into the college life and begin making more decisions for yourself.

The order of the book's sections was designed to cover issues in the order of importance or the order in which they might arise in your college path. After you begin college and you face some of the issues addressed here, it might be helpful to reread the applicable chapters. You can use this book as a guide before and during your freshman year, so keep it handy. You may not have roommate issues the first semester and you may not be faced with financial decisions right away, but chances are you will encounter many, if not all, of the topics covered in this book at some time during your freshman year.

College should be one of the happiest times in your life. You should meet new friends, experience new things, and, of course, study more than you ever thought possible. Ultimately, I hope you find the information contained in this book to be helpful to you as you begin and successfully complete your freshman year.

Transitioning from High School to College

You should be congratulated on your accomplishment in graduating from high school. Although it might be nice to sit back, relax, and enjoy this success, college-bound graduates do not have such a luxury. With the college semester looming ahead, there will be much to do before school starts again, and this time, school will be different. You were a senior in high school. You were the top dog. You are now moving from owning the school and knowing all the students, teachers, and classrooms to knowing few people at best, navigating a new campus, and adjusting to a whole new style of school. This transition can be scary, but with the tips in this book, you will learn what you need to know to make your changes go as smoothly as possible.

The first three chapters will cover some issues you may face as you transition from high school to college and will also offer tips and advice to successfully navigate through this new period. College life can be the best years of your life, but it can also be intimidating and scary at the beginning. With a little preparation and the tips offered in this book, you can enjoy your first year of college and jump-start a successful and rewarding college life. The following chapters also will remind you that your transition into college affects you, of course, but it also affects your family and friends. Realizing that everyone is facing major changes will help make it smoother for all those involved.

CHAPTER 1

Little Man, Big Campus

As they say, you are not in Kansas anymore. College is not high school. Gone are the days of knowing all your classmates, having all your classes in one building, knowing your teacher's first name, and being able to pick on the younger students. You have just been thrown into a new world — one where you are the bottom of the totem pole. In high school, younger students used to look to you to set trends and take the lead. Now you are wandering around just trying to find where Building 505 Classroom 302 is so you are not late to freshman algebra; do not worry. Every college senior was once a college freshman. You will make it through just as they did. Just be prepared for some bumpy roads, and hang on for the ride.

New Freedom Equals New Responsibility

Unless you are attending a local college and living at home, gone are the days of Mom and Dad watching over you. You will not have a nightly curfew, home-cooked meals, and Mom nagging you about whether you finished your homework or studied for the big test tomorrow. Although you may be thinking, "Woo-hoo, no more rules," bear in mind that with this newfound freedom comes new responsibility. You now will have to set your own rules. You will have to make sure you study for that test, complete your homework assignments, and get in bed early enough to make your 7 a.m. class (if you are crazy or unlucky enough to have a class at that hour). If you have lived most of your life under the strict rule of parents, you may be tempted to let loose completely and to do all the things your parents told you not to do, all in the first week of school. Do not do it. Although you certainly will take part in some things your parents shunned, whether it be staying out too late or drinking with your new friends, there will be plenty of time to "misbehave" in your college life. Take the first few weeks, even months, to get accustomed to college life. Relax a bit and enjoy the new freedoms without setting yourself up to become a first-semester dropout.

For students living at home and attending college locally, things will change as well. Rules will most likely be relaxed, and college professors, unlike high school teachers, will not be watching over you to make sure you do your best in their class. You will have to make sure you are getting the most out of your college experience, both scholastically and socially. Depending on the situation, you may be expected to pay rent or do more chores to maintain your living-at-home status. Your parents may not want to relinquish control, because you are still living under their roof. You may need to initiate a conversation to lay some ground rules for you and your parents so you can begin establishing your individuality as a college freshman. Talk to your parents about loosening or getting rid of curfews. Ask them what they expect of you while you are in college. Are good grades a trade for living at home? Will you be expected to maintain the same chores you might have had while you were in high school? What, if anything, will they be paying for while you are in school? What will you be expected to pay for? And perhaps most important, will Mom still be cooking dinner for you every night?

In the months or weeks before college, it is important to reflect on the upcoming changes. Think about what will change both in your life and the lives of those close to you. Find an outlet for your emotions. Many professionals suggest journaling in times of transition, such as leaving for college. You may find it helpful to write down your emotions and feelings and also your excitements and fears. If journaling works well for you or if you think it might, buy a new journal. Make sure it is symbolic or special to you in some way. This journal will be with you throughout college (depending on how much you write), so pick one that you are going to like for a few years to come. Be completely open and honest in your journal. Write down all your fears, anxieties, and dreams. Do not censor your journal. Your journal should be the one place you can say anything you want to and anything you feel. Warning: Having a journal runs the risk of someone else finding, reading, and spreading it. Keep your journal locked up in a safe place, unless you want the whole dorm floor to know your innermost thoughts.

Journaling is not the answer for everyone. You may find nature and meditation a good way to get in touch with your feelings and reflect on your upcoming change. Take a hike. If nature relaxes you or helps you focus, then get out there. Others will find that exercise is the best cure. You might feel your thoughts are most focused when pounding away on the treadmill or StairMaster®. Whatever your outlet, find something to help you deal with this major change in your life. Ignoring it or pushing your feelings aside will lead to pent-up stress and may result in a breakdown.

If you just rolled your eyes and debated putting this book down because I just "went there," recall the high dropout rate of college freshmen. If that is not enough to convince you that you need to find an outlet for your stress, think of Britney Spears and her breakdown. I will bet she did not journal, turn to nature, or exercise her stress away. Do not be Britney. Find a positive outlet, whatever that may be, and use it. Built-up stress cannot only cause nervous breakdowns, but also serious health issues. Some students gain weight (and with the already high chances of "the freshman 15," you do not need more reasons to eat), some experience high blood pressure, and some will suffer from severe headaches. The list of health concerns goes on, but you get the point. Deal with your stress in a productive manner.

College provides an excellent opportunity to learn about the world and about you. Do not confine yourself to what you have always done. Step outside of your comfort zone. Try new things. Make new friends. Be open-minded to new ideas and philosophies. Do not be too quick to judge, and do not hang out with people just because they seem most like you or remind you of your high school buddies. College is a time to experience new things and test your boundaries and limitations. Do not worry if you make mistakes. Everyone will slip and fall at some point in life. If you fail a test, make a bad decision, or date the wrong person, tomorrow is a new day. With each day, you decide what path your life will take. Pick yourself up and move on.

Setting Goals and Staying Focused

Bear in mind that college is a marathon, not a sprint. Do not burn yourself out in your first year. Do not overload on classes or take the hardest classes back to back. Be realistic about yourself and your limitations. Stay focused on the finish line (that is, graduation), and set small goals to get you through each year, each semester, and even each day. That is the best way to stay on track and keep your focus. This may sound "cheesy;" it may seem a little too much like some fluffy high school assignment, but it works. This advice comes highly recommended by many professionals, counselors, and psychologists.

Before heading to college, take some time to think about why you are going to college. Ask yourself what you expect to get out of college besides a piece of paper after four years. Think about where you want to see yourself after graduation. You do not have to have all the answers. You do not have to know what your major will be or the career path you want to take when you are finished with school. Many freshmen who think they have all the answers end up changing their minds while in school anyway. Do not worry if you do not know. Your goals may be as broad as getting through school and making new friends. You might want to study abroad one year or join a fraternity or sorority. Whatever you goals are, knowing them ahead of time and putting them on paper as a reminder will help lead to success in your freshman year and in your college experience as a whole.

Write down a list of your goals. Keep the list handy so when things get rough and you are not sure why you are staying in college or went to college in the first place, you can pull out that list and re-motivate yourself. Remind yourself why you are working so hard, and think of how rewarding the outcome will be. If you are proud of your goals and not shy about such things, have your goals list laminated and hang it on the wall of your dorm room. Otherwise, print it out on a small sheet of paper and carry it in your wallet or purse. Use whatever method works best for you, but make sure you have your goals list handy at all times.

Case Study: Transitioning Challenges

Alan Acosta, Residence Coordinator
University Housing, Florida State University

Alan Acosta said the biggest challenge for most freshmen is making the transition from living at home to living on their own. He said many first-year students are unequipped to handle doing many basic things for themselves, such as doing laundry, cooking a meal, cleaning their room, or even waking up in time to go to class.

But more important than that, many students struggle with being separated from their family or friends. First-year students, particularly during the first few months of the year, will go home every weekend to maintain that connection. Staying close to home has become even easier with cell phones and online social networks such as Facebook and MySpace®, but students should realize that finding a social support network at the university is extremely important.

Acosta said students having the freedom to make their own decisions often provides the most temptations while they are at college. They are free to make choices without anyone telling them what they should and should not do. Most students are not ready for that level of freedom when they get to college and can end up making some bad choices. Parents should try to prepare their child to be ready to make good decisions and avoid the usual temptations that many college students face, he said.

Eric Booth, M.A., Director of Residence Life
University of Texas-Pan American

Eric Booth said the biggest challenges freshmen face are dependency issues, peer pressure, acceptance, and study habits. He also said alcohol and drugs tempt those freshman living on campus because of their new independence. For freshmen to successfully navigate through their first year of school, Booth said they should develop strong study habits early. He also said freshmen should understand the value of respect for other students, staff,

Case Study: Transitioning Challenges

and professors. Freshmen should get to know other students and the faculty and work at cultivating those relationships during their time in college.

Kelly R. Doel, Area Coordinator
University of Central Florida

Kelly Doel said she recognizes that freshmen face many challenges, one of which is learning how to handle their newfound independence. She said freshmen can have difficultly learning how to balance an academic and social life. Peer pressure to experiment with alcohol and drugs can also be challenging for first-year college students.

Freedoms such as choosing to socialize rather than study and partying are the most tempting to freshmen, according to Doel. Parents are not there to supervise behavior, so freshmen can find it easy to make bad choices. There are no immediate consequences for not studying, not doing laundry, not coming home by a certain time, or sleeping in late instead of going to class.

To be successful the first year of college, Doel said freshmen must find a balance in their life. Developing time-management skills and establishing realistic goals are incredibly helpful in assisting students to stay focused. Doel also recommended students surround themselves with positive influences and people who are supportive of their goals.

Doel said incoming freshmen should talk to people they know in college to get an idea of what to expect. Students should seek mentors who have accomplished the same goals they wish to accomplish. Looking at the college or university's Web site to learn about clubs and organizations can also give students an idea of how to get involved on campus before arriving there.

Jay Goodman, Graduate
Pennsylvania State University

Jay Goodman said every freshman has to discover and learn from his or her own challenges. He recalled that his biggest challenge as a college freshman was learning how to study. He breezed through high school with a 4.0 grade point

Case Study: Transitioning Challenges

average (GPA) or better, but he did not have to work hard to get those grades. Goodman said he had a rude awakening during his first college semester.

Not only was he thrown into the mix of difficult engineering "weed-out" courses, he said, nothing was coming as naturally as it had before. He struggled to discover a studying and note-taking method that worked for him.

At large schools, Goodman says freshmen might have a tendency to skip class because they can skip without the professor noticing and without their grades being directly docked. Large classes make attendance meaningless in the eyes of professors. He warns that even though freshmen can skip class without a professor's knowing or even caring, they will eventually find out their final grade is negatively affected from all the material they missed in class.

For freshmen to stay focused, Goodman recommended that they identify distractions and eliminate them as soon as possible, although this is easier said than done. If distractions cannot be eliminated, he said, freshmen should at least keep their distractions moderated. He advised that if freshmen cannot identify their own distractions, they should ask their roommates to tell them what they see as their biggest distraction. An outside eye can often see what one cannot identify for oneself, he said.

Ashley Chittum, Sophomore
Tennessee Wesleyan College

Ashley Chittum said her two biggest challenges when she started her freshman year were learning how to study for college exams and learning how to manage her time without having her parents around. She said she thinks the biggest temptation freshmen face is whether to party or study.

Carolynn S. Nath, Area Coordinator
University of Central Florida

Carolynn Nath said freshmen need to learn time-management skills. Students not having an adult around telling them what to do might struggle with managing their own time. Conversely, if students do have someone calling them often, they might want to express themselves by doing it "their own way" despite a parent's

Case Study: Transitioning Challenges

recommendations. Students should plan for courses accordingly. If they are not used to having a "block" schedule in high school, she said it is much harder for them to transition to having courses three days, two days, or one day a week for 60 minutes to three hours at a time.

A student's social priorities can also be challenging to freshmen, Nath said. Whether a student's social life is empty or full, students often struggle to find a middle ground. Some of the other new freedoms that present challenges to freshmen, according to Nath, include having no curfew, no one telling them to stay on task and do homework, and having a new type of social life. She said students will have the opportunity to enjoy fun new things or places such as clubs and organizations on campus, dance clubs, bars (coffee, hookah, alcoholic, and oxygen, just to name a few), strip clubs, theme parks (season passes), and other recreational areas (ski slopes, beaches, lakes, and sand dunes, for example). Nath suggested students try and stick to joining one or two organizations or clubs at most in their freshman year and should wait until their sophomore year to hold a position in them.

Other distractions freshmen face include exploring their new community. Nath said older and local students can show new freshmen around the community. This opportunity may be exciting in a larger or smaller city with a variety of sites to explore. If a student has a vehicle, Nath said, he or she might indulge in road trips on the weekend and enjoy taking spring break vacations. Even those students without vehicles will be able to ride with friends for weekend road trips and little vacations.

With all these new opportunities and freedoms that freshmen face, she said freshmen should focus on the goal of graduation and organizations that will be supportive of that goal.

Freshmen should learn to enjoy themselves but know their limits. Even with their new busy schedules, Nath said freshmen will have a significant amount of free time but students need to realize that they are in college to study and should not play the entire time.

Case Study: Transitioning Challenges

When it comes to other advice for incoming freshmen, Nath said, "Do not believe what you see in the movies." She explained that movie depictions of college are not what college is or should be about. Although freshmen will have fun, they need to think of every penny that is being spent on classes and what could be done with all that money. Do some math and calculate the cost of one course (each credit is work x amount + the cost of books), and divide it by the number of class sessions in each course. She said this amount is how much students or whoever is paying for the student's education will be losing if a student misses just one class. Freshmen should ask themselves two questions before they skip a class: What is that worth to you or the person is paying?, and would you be willing to reimburse the person paying for the cost of the class if you missed one?

Ultimately, Nath said students need to understand that going to college is a privilege many people would love to have, so they should embrace the opportunity.

Matthew Gramling, Sophomore
Oglethorpe College

Matthew Gramling said one of his challenges as a freshman was adjusting to living in a large city, because he came from a small town. He also said he had trouble finding people that he got along with well at first, but then he made many friends shortly after starting school. During his first semester, Gramling came home most weekends, but by the second semester his weekend visits home were far less frequent. In his experience, during the first two weeks on campus, everybody talked to everybody, but he said that began to stop as groups of friends started forming. He also struggled with not fitting in because of his faith. As a strong Christian, Gramling sometimes felt singled out, as most of his classmates were agnostic or atheist. After his campus Bible study started and he found academic groups to join, Gramling felt much more comfortable with his new environment.

Gramling said he sees "getting drunk off your butt all the time" as one of the biggest temptations that most of his classmates faced as freshmen in college, because no matter what age you are, getting alcohol while in college

Case Study: Transitioning Challenges

is easy. Gramling advised freshmen to get their work done first and then do other things like socializing with friends. If freshmen finish their assignments ahead of time, they will have more free time to hang out with friends or go to parties.

Frederica Anderson, Sophomore
Savannah College of Art and Design

Frederica Anderson said the biggest challenge freshmen face in their first year of college is adjusting to the amount and level or work assigned in college courses. She said they also struggle with adjusting to the time they are given to complete this workload. When it comes to freedoms that present challenges to freshmen, Anderson said parties, drinking, and relationships (especially because they are no longer under the watchful eyes of their parents) top the list of temptations freshmen will face. Freshmen should try to adjust to their new lifestyle, freedoms, and workload as quickly as they can. Midterms will roll around fast, especially for students on the quarter system, and freshmen need to stay on top of the workload from the beginning. Before moving in and beginning college, Anderson advised that students be mentally prepared and plan for their upcoming class schedule and move-in day well ahead of time.

James John, Professional Student
Georgia Highlands College

The biggest challenge James John faced was how to balance himself. He said he was a freshman in college at only 17 years old and tended to party more and study less. He was more focused on work at that time because work was an immediate gratification, whereas school is a long-term goal. As a freshman, John found the free time the hardest temptation for him to deal with. He often asked himself, "Why go to school at 8 a.m. when I can just skip it and sleep in?" When it comes to advice for freshmen, John said, "Study." Students should spend the first year of college trying to better understand their specific studying style. He said that high schools around the nation do not adequately prepare a student for college. One last word of advice: "Enjoy your first year, but not too much."

Case Study: Transitioning Challenges

Ryan Thompson, 2008 Graduate
Southern Polytechnic State University

Understanding diversity is a challenge freshman face during their first year of college, according to Ryan Thompson. He recalled how some students had issues adapting to different peoples' backgrounds in the dorms. Some of his friends would complain about how their roommates were when it came to responsibility in the dorm.

Thompson said the new freedom of having no parents around and no one making decisions for students but themselves presents a temptation for college freshmen to go against the teachings or advice of their parents. Thompson said the key things freshmen need to remember to survive their first year of college include:

- Stay focused on the goal

- Plan ahead

- Be open-minded and not judgmental

- Communicate with professors

- Develop friends or have a social outlet

- Do not get stressed by taking on too much

- Maintain a balance for managing school, personal life, family, and work

He said the best advice for an incoming freshman is to get involved and embark on meeting different types of people. Some students will have the urge to communicate only with their old clique from high school and not meet new people, but meeting individuals from different backgrounds will help prepare students for the different types of personalities and characteristics of people in the "real" world.

Creating Your Own Mission Statement

Successfully navigating through college is best accomplished by having clearly defined goals. But what do those goals mean? After you have some goals outlined, blend them together, delve a little deeper, and create your own personal mission statement. Think of it like a business plan for your college life. It is almost a motto but not as catchy and almost certainly a little longer. Your mission statement should be your words to live by while you are in school.

Ask yourself some questions: What is most important to you in your college life? What is it you most want to accomplish in your four years of school? Academics, of course, should be of high importance in your college life. But there is more to college than making good grades. College is a time of meeting new friends, trying new things, and discovering new aspects of yourself.

The following questions can be used to create your own personal mission statement:

- What expectations do you have for your college experience?

- What experiences and knowledge do you hope to gain while in college?

- Are you planning on attending graduate school? If so, what do you need to accomplish in college to help realize that goal?

- What are your life aspirations?

Use the answers to these questions along with your list of goals to write about four sentences for your mission statement. Do not be afraid to aim high, and be honest about your goals for your life. It may be helpful to share your mission statement with one or two people closest to you. Ask them if they feel your mission statement reflects your beliefs and dreams. After you feel happy with your statement, keep a copy somewhere to remind yourself. Keep it in your wallet or post it in your dorm room. If you ever should get off track, read your mission statement again. Keep your mission statement and your goals list close to each other. They should play off each other well. If there are large discrepancies between the two, you may need to go back and reevaluate one or the other.

Your goals will change throughout your life and most likely even throughout your college career. As your goals change, so will your mission statement. This statement is intended to guide you on a path to graduation and to attaining the things you want most out of your college experience and your life. Feel free to edit or entirely rewrite your statement as often as you feel necessary. This is not to say that you should be rewriting your goals on a daily basis. Your freshman year in college can be quite emotionally draining, and some days you might feel as though you want to change everything, only to wake up the next morning and discount everything you thought the day before. Give yourself some time to truly change, and when those changes happen, go back and rewrite your goals and mission statement.

Size Does Matter

Whether the college you are attending is a small campus or a gigantic state university, the size of their new college campus intimidates most students. In high school, all your classes were in one building. In college, that is rarely the case. Depending on the size of your college or university, you may have a 30-minute walk between classes. Although you have to take into consideration you will need to leave earlier for classes, the deeper issue lies in the intimidation a campus can have for a freshman.

No matter the size of the campus, it is almost definite that it will be larger than your high school. Visit your college ahead of time. Your college will hold a freshman orientation. Be sure to attend and pay attention to the campus layout, which building your classes will mostly be held in, and, perhaps most important, the location of the cafeteria and other key hot spots. After you have your schedule, find where your classes are before the first day of school. You do not want to be frantically searching the campus for your first class and showing up late the first day of school. Although this may be understandable, it can be embarrassing.

Case Study: Getting Lost and Using Campus Landmarks

Eric Chaney, 2002 Graduate
University of Missouri-Columbia

When Eric Chaney first started college, the campus seemed huge, and he was constantly getting lost, especially if he had been doing any "barroom studying." At the University of Missouri-Columbia campus, the administration building named Jesse Hall had a huge dome on top, visible from anywhere on campus.

So Eric made it a point to learn the route home from Jesse to his dorm. If he was ever lost on campus, three sheets to the wind or not, all he had to do was find that huge white dome and make his way toward it. After he got there, he knew the way home.

Case Study: Getting Lost and Using Campus Landmarks

Alan Acosta, Residence Coordinator
University Housing, Florida State University

According to Alan Acosta, "Clearly the size of a campus is a big issue (no pun intended)." He said one issue related to size is that students attending small colleges tend to feel as if they know everyone, whereas students at large universities sometimes feel as if they are just another number at the institution. Students who are at large universities, he said, must find ways to bring the university down to a size they can handle. He suggested students get involved in clubs and organizations, make new friends, and, if they live in a residence hall, get involved in their floor or hall community.

Conversely, Acosta said, a student at a small school can feel like everyone at the institution knows their issues or problems, unlike a student in a large university who can maintain privacy. Although Acosta said this can be difficult to overcome for students at a small college, a strong circle of friends can help.

Eric Booth, M.A., Director of Residence Life
University of Texas-Pan American

Eric Booth said college students at small schools struggle with the lack of anonymity due to fewer students. Other issues students at small schools face, according to Booth, include rising college costs and a lack of academic options.

Kelly R. Doel, Area Coordinator
University of Central Florida

Kelly Doel said students attending small colleges may feel as if they are still in high school, and a small campus may not offer as many courses, professors, or majors. These students might not have as many clubs and organizations to pick from, and the campus may not offer as much of a diverse learning experience. On the other hand, Doel acknowledged that students attending large universities may find it difficult to feel connected on campus because there are so many choices. Students feel like a number due to large classes and completing most processes online. Another issue students at large campuses face, according to Doel, is it might be much more difficult to obtain on-campus housing.

Case Study: Getting Lost and Using Campus Landmarks

Jay Goodman, Graduate
Pennsylvania State University

Jay Goodman said large schools are extremely impersonal. Freshmen attending large schools need to get used to large classes. His freshman calculus classes had more than 600 students, and his general education economics course had a whopping 1,200 students. With classes that large, Goodman said professors do not know each student and will not recall every freshman, even those who stay after class and chat with them on occasion. He advised, "Do not take it personally." One-on-one access to the professor in a large school, according to Goodman, is hard to come by in freshman classes. He does not recall talking to professors until he was in his 300 level courses (or, his junior year). Freshmen in large classes truly are just another number.

Ashley Chittum, Sophomore
Tennessee Wesleyan College

Ashley Chittum advised students attending both small and large colleges to find their classes ahead of time and map out a routine before classes start. Being familiar with the campus, no matter what the size, will help freshmen feel more comfortable after classes start.

Carolynn S. Nath, Area Coordinator
University of Central Florida

Carolyn Nath said small institutions may be compared or be exceedingly similar to high school. Students will know their professors by name and likely know every student in each of their classes. She said students at small schools will be noticed when absent and/or present, will get the attention needed, and will be challenged on an individual basis.

At large institutions, Nath said the stigma is students are a just number. She said in most cases students are just a number until they begin in their major classes, because general education requirement courses may have more than 200 people in each class. After students have been accepted into their major (students may have to apply for specific fields), they will have smaller courses with five to 30 students (depending on the program).

Case Study: Getting Lost and Using Campus Landmarks

Frederica Anderson, Sophomore
Savannah College of Art and Design

Frederica Anderson said students at small or large universities might struggle with adjusting to living in cramped co-ed dorms (with three or four classmates in one area). She said students at large universities will face large classrooms and hundreds of students in one class. At a small campus, students might find a limited selection of courses offered or a limited selection of times that each course is available.

James John, Professional Student
Georgia Highlands College

James John said community colleges are more relaxed and students can flow with professors into a subject. Universities are more like a huge machine, churning out graduates as soon as possible, according to John.

Ryan Thompson, 2008 Graduate
Southern Polytechnic State University

Ryan Thompson said small colleges are geared more toward a one-on-one interaction with professors, and students may face fewer challenges. Larger universities, he said, characteristically have massive classroom populations where the students could begin to feel as if they are just another number. He said students who are accustomed to smaller high schools might have a hard time adapting to larger universities.

CHAPTER 2

Shipping Out: Leaving Home

Leaving home may feel like the hardest thing about going to college, or it may feel like the biggest advantage. Either way, leaving home will be a huge change for you and for those closest to you. Your family and friends will be facing an emotional transition as you leave. Being mindful of your feelings and also the feelings of your loved ones will help ease the transition for all involved.

Saying Goodbye

Depending on how close you are to your family and friends, saying goodbye might be one of the most difficult things you face when leaving for college. Despite how much or little you think you will miss your parents, almost everyone will experience some form of homesickness. Even those who cannot wait to get out of the house and away from annoying siblings and overbearing parents will have times when they will miss home. There are sure to be evenings when you are sitting alone in your dorm room wondering what is going on back home. You might even start missing those annoying things your parents and siblings used to do. Plus, because life at home moves on without you there, you may start to feel lonely and not important to them anymore.

Combat homesickness by bringing home to you. That does not mean asking your mom to drive to campus every time you miss her. Also, if you are attending college far from home, you cannot ask your whole family to move to another state just to be closer to you while you are in school. But it is important to not forget to stay connected to family and friends back home while also setting boundaries and establishing your own individuality. You also need to realize you are not the only one saying goodbye. If you are the first of your siblings to move away from home, the transition will be even harder on your family. And no matter what, your friends will miss you. Being understanding of the changes your family and friends are going through will help ease the transition for all of you.

Your Parents

Of course, your parents will be facing a big change as you head off to college. They may be supporting you financially in your college life, whether through loans or helping to cover your living expenses. Be sensitive to the fact that they have an interest in your success. Plus, you are their "baby," and now you are all grown up. They may even cry, so be prepared. Before you leave for school, schedule some alone time with your parents. Whether you plan a fishing trip with your dad or coffee with your mom, be sure to spend some time with them before you go. Yes, you will still see them after you leave, but it will mean so much to them (and maybe even to you) to share some quality time before you go. "Quality time" may seem cliché or even a bit lame, but it will help ease the transition for them. It may help them not cry as much when they drop you off at school.

When you spend time with your parents before you leave, ask them for advice, and listen to the advice they give you. They may have attended college during the Stone Age, but some advice still applies. You may be surprised by what you learn. Maybe your mom was in a sorority and can give you advice on the benefits of joining one yourself. Or maybe your dad played sports in college and you are too. He might have some excellent tips on juggling sports, scholastics, and a social life. Even if your parents do not have college stories that will help you, or even if they did not attend college, listen to what they have to say. They will feel better for having had the chance to give you last-minute pointers before you go. Your parents will be a quality support system while you are in school. Having the lines of communication open before you leave will help make it easier to talk to them after you are facing challenges in school. Tell them your own fears about college. Share with them any of the possible insecurities you may have about your first year.

Case Study: Parental Advice

Elizabeth Boyle, 1999 Graduate
North Carolina State University

Elizabeth Boyle said her father put down two rules for her before she could go off to college. Rule No. 1 was, learn to touch type — no hunting and pecking allowed. Rule No. 2 was learn to drive a stick shift car.

She recalled fighting her father about these rules, with pleas of "Why would I ever need to drive a stick shift?" and "This computer thing will never catch on, and besides that, I have my own way of typing." When she figured out he was quite serious, she did learn both and then went off to school on schedule.

Much to her dismay, she recalled that during her first weekend at school, she found rule number two quite handy. She was at a party in an unfamiliar apartment belonging to a group of boys. She was the only one who had not been drinking heavily, and by the end of the night, she said she and her friends wanted to head back to the dorm. The problem was none of her girlfriends had a car. They

> ## Case Study: Parental Advice
>
> found a guy willing to let them drive his car to a parking lot between school and his apartment, but, of course, it was a stick shift. (As luck would have it for Boyle.)
>
> So, Boyle drove the guy's stick shift car, which, thanks to her dad's rule, she knew how to drive. She said they fit an extremely large man in the front seat and five people in the back seat of this tiny hatchback and got safely home. To this day, Boyle has not told her dad about this story for fear that she may never stop hearing the phrase, "I told you so."

Your Siblings

If you are the oldest child or first to leave for college, you should schedule some time with your siblings before you head out. Your younger brother or sister might be annoying you now, but maintaining a close relationship with your siblings is important; you are a role model to them. They look up to you, so spend some one-on-one time before you go. If you have older siblings who are already in college, ask them to go to lunch with you one afternoon. Ask them what they recall of their freshman year in college. Listen to their advice and try to learn from any mistakes they might have made in their first year of school.

Some colleges offer "little siblings" weekends where the little sisters and brothers of students can come and stay overnight and participate in special activities. This can be a great bonding time for siblings and will be something that younger siblings will be very excited about. If your school doesn't have this program, talk to your resident assistant and see if you could arrange to have your sibling spend the weekend with you anyway.

Your Friends

Have a party. Most high school seniors hold a graduation party, but you may want to hold a going-away-to-college party as well. Invite over all your high school friends or plan to meet them all at your favorite local hangout spot. Not only is going to college a good excuse for a party, but it will serve as a good way to say goodbye to all your friends in one sweep; plus, parties are fun. So, send out an Evite (**www.evite.com**) or text message to all your friends and celebrate your leaving for college. Be sure, if you do not already have a list, to get everyone's e-mail addresses before you go. You will want to be able to keep contact with your high school buddies while you are in college.

Packing

Visit your dorm room before moving day. If your college is too far away to visit, talk to your advisor about the size (or lack thereof) of your dorm room. If you are able to do so, talk to your roommate or roommates before you pack. Certain items such as TVs and small fridges can be shared. Also, be sure to check out your college's unapproved items list. Certain appliances, such as microwaves, hot plates, and even coffee makers may not be allowed by your school; find out before you go what items you cannot take. You do not want to get caught at school with a bunch of items you cannot have and be forced to ship them all home in the first week; shipping is expensive and a hassle. Finding out what you can and cannot bring before you get there will help the move be smoother and save room in the van.

The following sections note must-haves, might-wants, and leave-at-home items. You might disagree with some of these items, or you might be adamant about bringing your prized baseball card collection, despite the fact that it is not recommend. Tailor these lists to your own needs and personality, but first, read through why such items are or are not on the list. There are reasons behind why certain items are on certain lists.

Must-Haves

Computer: Although most college campuses have computer labs, if possible, bring your own. You do not want to have to wait for a computer when you actually need one, be limited in the hours you can access a computer, or be confined to doing all your computer work in the computer lab. Having your own computer will give you unlimited access to your files. You will not have to make sure you have your flash drive with you as you head out to the lab. You will not even have to go to the computer lab. If you do invest in your own computer, most college students prefer laptops to desktops. With a laptop, you can study wherever you need to, be it your room, the library, a local café, or even in the park. Make sure your laptop has a wireless Internet card, either external or internal. Having your own computer will also make it easier to store your school files (as opposed to a flash drive), keep pictures from home, and check your e-mail at your convenience.

It is important to find out if your school has any requirements or recommendations on the type of software your computer should have installed and if they require you to have a PC or a Mac. Make sure that you also check the requirements with your major, as different majors require different software. Also, it is a good idea to see what type of Internet connection you will be using in your dorm room or apartment so you can make sure you have the necessary equipment and cables. Also, be aware of your school's Internet policy. In the past, students have received major fines for music piracy. Be sure to understand what you can and cannot download from the Internet at school.

- **Flip-flops and shower bag:** If you have a community shower, you will want to wear flip-flops — both to and from the shower and in the shower, unless of course, foot fungus and warts sound like fun to you. If you have to walk down the hall to get to the shower, having a waterproof shower bag or basket with all your showering needs will make the walk easier. If you have a shower in your room and share it with more than one roommate, you may also want a shower bag. There may not be space in the shower to leave your shampoo and conditioner, plus you run the risk of roommates using your supplies.

- **Clothes:** Obviously, you are not planning on attending college in the buff, but make sure you bring an adequate and appropriate supply of clothing. If you attended high school in Florida but will be going to college in Colorado, you may need to go shopping. Bringing tank tops and shorts may not be helpful in Colorado in September, so pack appropriately. Although you cannot bring your whole wardrobe with you, you need to bring enough clothes to not have to do laundry every other day. Laundry will be expensive, and honestly, it can be a pain. Also, it is always a good idea to pack extra socks and underwear.

- **Clothes hamper:** There are many choices of clothes hampers. Pick one that can hold a good amount of dirty clothes without taking up too much room and that will be easy to carry when you are doing laundry. A collapsible hamper may come in handy while carrying it empty back to your room after throwing your clothes in the washing machine.

- **Storage bins:** To judge your storage needs, see your room beforehand or talk to someone about your room. Find storage bins that can fit under the bed or stack neatly in your closet.

- **Music:** Do not bring your entire CD collection. Bring an MP3 player and dock. Having your favorite hits should not take up half of your dorm room.

- **A touch of home:** The key word here is "touch." Do not bring every picture you have of your high school friends or all the posters from your room at home. Pick a few things to take to remind you of home and to personalize your dorm room. Be selective, though, with which keepsakes you choose to take with you, and bear in mind that your dorm room is not much larger than a tissue box, and you will not be the only one living in it.

- **First-aid kit:** You do not need to bring your mom's entire medicine cabinet. At least pack bandages and some headache medicine.

- **Alarm clock:** Whether your first class is at 7 a.m. or noon, you will need an alarm clock to make sure you are awake in time. Make sure you get one with battery backup and that you put batteries in it. College professors will not care about any excuse.

- **Backpack:** Unless you want to have shoulder and back problems in your 30s, do not be cheap with your backpack. College books are much heavier than your high school textbooks. Check out such brands as Columbia®, L.L. Bean, Jansport®, and North Face. It is best to look at backpacks in the stores and find the model you like the most. Then, write down the brand, model number, and price; go home, get online, and start searching for the best deal.

- **Cell phone or calling card:** Most high school seniors already have cell phones — even some elementary students have cell phones. If somehow you are rebelling against technology or still believe cell phones cause brain tumors, at least get a calling card. Unless you are going to school locally, you will want an easy way to make long-distance calls home. Do not forget the charger.

- **Day planner or organizer:** Time management might be one of the most important factors in successfully completing your freshman year of college. Get a day planner or organizer that works for you. Be sure it has enough room to write in daily class schedules, homework assignments, and social events.

- **Address book or list:** Before you leave for college, start gathering phone numbers, addresses, and e-mail addresses of family and friends that you will want to maintain contact with while you are at school. An excellent starting point is using the list of people you sent graduation invites to. When you hold any graduation parties or pre-college fiestas, pass around your address book.

- **Bedding and pillow(s):** Make sure you know the size of the bed in your dorm room before you buy sheets, because some beds in dorm rooms are longer than normal twin beds. Consider getting some good-quality sheets. If you decide to spend a few extra bucks (or a few extra bucks of your parents' money) to invest in quality sheets, look for some with high thread counts. The higher the thread count, the better quality and the softer the sheets. As a college freshman, sleep will be important, and although you may not get enough of it as you would like, you will want to be as comfortable as possible.

- **Cleaning supplies:** Do not be voted messiest dorm room. It is not a good reputation to have and may hinder your dating ability. Buy some basic cleaning supplies such as a broom and all-purpose cleaner and a sponge, dish soap, or scrub brush for washing dishes.

- **Dishes, glasses, and coffee mug:** Chances are you will either get tired of cafeteria food or want some late-night snacks when nothing is open. Having a handful of basic, easy-to-cook food items in your dorm room will be a lifesaver for late-night study sessions and mornings when you barely have time to eat breakfast while running to your first class.

Might-Wants

Board games and cards: Cards are perfect. They are small, offer many choices in games and can be played with as few as, well, just one. You may want to bring a favorite board game. A frisbee is also a great item to bring as there is no limit to how many people can play and it is a great way to meet neighbors. Games can be excellent ways to blow off steam after a big test and can be perfect icebreakers with your new roommate(s) and neighbors.

Allowed appliances: If your college allows these items, you may want to bring them along: a microwave, coffee maker, toaster, hot plate, George Foreman grill, and an iron. If you cannot bring a hot plate, check with your college's housing department to see if you can bring a crock pot.

Bed Risers: These can be helpful to create more space under your bed for extra storage. You should check with your housing department or apartment manager to see if the beds in your room are compatible with bed risers.

Desk lamp: Some sources suggest halogen lamps are the best because the softer light is easier on the eyes. Just make sure that halogen lamps are not on the unapproved items list for your school. Either way, you will need a desk lamp. It will help for any late-night study sessions when your roommate is already asleep.

Rug: If your dorm room or apartment is not carpeted, you may way to bring a floor rug to make your space more livable. Check with your housing department or apartment manager to see if your room is carpeted and if not, what size the room is.

Guitar: If you play the guitar, bring it. It can be a good outlet for dealing with stress and is a wonderful conversation starter. You will be able to entertain your new friends, roommates, and, of course, your dates. If your guitar is expensive or has an especially important sentimental value, be sure you think ahead about security. Even if you would trust your roommate with it, you may not trust everyone else who might be in and out of your room.

Sewing kit: Even if you have never used one and do not think you ever will, sewing kits are small and can come in handy. Your kit should include buttons, safety pins, sewing needles, and thread.

TV and DVD player: If your roommate is not already bringing one or both, you will most likely want some way to watch television and movies in the comfort of your dorm room.

Dry-erase board: These are good for leaving messages to roommates and writing out grocery lists as you run out of things. You will not need four of them though, so talk to your roommate before you buy this as well.

Bicycle: If your campus is large and designed for easy bike access, you might want to bring your ten-speed along. Bikes can serve as a mode of transportation on and off campus and also as a form of exercise (which you will need to avoid the freshman 15 mentioned later in this book). Before you decide whether to bring your bike, ask your advisor about how bike-friendly your campus is and also about bike security. Sometimes, bikes are stolen even if they have locks on them, and certain colleges have a higher prevalence of bike thefts than others.

Journal: If you decide journaling is a good outlet for you, bring one along. Find a journal that is easy enough to carry around so that you can journal in between classes or when sitting in the park on a nice day.

Leave at Home

Jumbo-sized anything: Although Mom may want to send you off prepared for the entire year of school with jumbo shampoos or 20 rolls of paper towels, there is just no room for it. Buy smaller sizes and restock often.

Your entire library, DVD collection, or photo albums: Again, there just is not space. Plus, you will be so busy with homework, hanging out with new friends, and studying like mad that you will not have time to reread all your favorite books, watch all your movies, and reminisce about home with your baby pictures. Select a few of your favorites, and leave the rest at home. You can always have your parents send a care package with things you forgot or switch out some movies on one of your visits home.

High school yearbooks: High school is over. Bring a few pictures of your best high school buddies, but leave the yearbooks at home. They will take up too much room, and to be honest, it is time to move on.

Out-of-season clothes: You will be moving into your dorm room around late August or early September. Research the weather of the local campus. If you are attending college in colder climates, it may still be warm when you move in. But the warm weather will not be lasting long. Pack clothing you can wear until the next season change. Do not bring your entire tank top collection for the chance it might be hot for a few days. You will not have room to store all your clothes, and you will be visiting home before summer rolls around again.

The kitchen sink: No, you would not truly plan on packing the kitchen sink, but I do have a point with this one: You cannot take everything with you. If you overpack, you not only will not have enough room to move around, but you will also most likely end up mailing stuff back home, which is inconvenient and can be expensive. Or you will be carrying it back to the car or driving it back home the following weekend. As you are packing, be honest about how often you will use an item, how much you need it, and if there is room for it.

CHAPTER 3

Home Again

It may seem premature to talk about visiting home when you have not even left for school, but now is the perfect time to schedule your visits. After you get to school, you might be tempted to run home at the first sign of homesickness. If you plan your visits home before you leave for school, you will be less tempted to run home because you miss your mom's cooking or you got in a fight with your roommate. Sticking it out through the tough times and learning to get along without running home will help you adjust to college life more quickly and help you bond with your new college friends. How close to home your school is and how close you are to your family will determine how often you visit home.

Holidays

Most college students will spend the holidays at home. Not only are most school breaks scheduled around the holidays, but these are also the best times to visit your family and friends. If your parents are divorced, you may want to schedule which holidays you will spend with which parent. Having a schedule in advance will help avoid hurt feelings or misunderstandings later on. Plan visits for Thanksgiving, Christmas, Hanukkah, Kwanza, New Year's Day, and Easter.

Care Packages

One of the best perks about leaving home for college is the care packages. Whether they include letters from home, your mom's homemade cookies, or drawings from younger siblings, care packages offer an excellent connection to home. When stress levels are high because of finals or roommate issues, care packages can brighten your day like nothing else. Print out labels with your dorm address and leave them at home for your mom and dad to easily mail out packages. Talk with them about what you would most like to see in a care package.

Here is a list of care package suggestions. Leave a copy at home for your mom or dad and highlight your favorites. Otherwise, you might end up with a bag of chips you do not like or toilet paper.

Care Package Suggestions

- Mom's homemade cookies (not only will you love them, but your roommate will love you for sharing them)

- Handwritten notes from family

- Your favorite author's latest book

- DVDs and CDs

- Magazines

- Your local newspaper

- Your favorite soap or body wash

- Ramen noodles — or not (If you like them, ask for them. If you are sick and tired of them or never saw the fascination in them, say so.)

- Snack foods. Be sure to include some healthy options, such as popcorn, and not the extra-butter kind. With late-night studying in your future, you will want some munchies, but you do not want your care package to add to your waistline.)

- Special toiletry items. If there are items that only a local shop sells or that might be a little too pricey for your college freshman budget, ask for it in your care packages.

Weekend Visits

If your college is close enough to home for weekend visits, you might plan some weekend trips home, or you might plan on going home almost every weekend. You can bring your laundry, get a home-cooked meal, and spend some time with family and friends. Just be sure you are not spending every weekend at home. Try to wait at least two months before you go home for the first time. By waiting, you will get more comfortable with your new school, life style, and friends. If you spend too many weekends at home, you may not get all the studying done that you have to do. You could be distracted by family and friends at home, and your grades may suffer. Of course, weekend visits can be wonderful. The advantages to weekend visits are that you can reconnect, do your laundry for free (and maybe even talk your mom or dad into doing your laundry for you), and get a break from cafeteria food.

Spring Break

Students choose to do different things during spring break. Be aware, however, that if you live in a dorm, the dorm may close during this week and you will be forced to go somewhere. Some students go home to visit family, while others choose to go on vacations with friends. If you decide on this route, remember to make smart decisions regarding alcohol, drugs, and sex. At many popular spring break locations, making poor decisions regarding these issues can lead to serious problems. You do not want to do something that you will regret later. There is definitely nothing wrong with having a good time with your friends on a tropical beach; however, everyone has heard stories of drug or alcohol overdoses, rapes, or arrests for under-age drinking.

You may want to consider a different alternative for a spring break location. Some schools have volunteer trips to other countries that students can participate in during the week of spring break. If you go home for spring break, you might want to take advantage of your time off by going on day trips, volunteering with a local organization, or just catching up with old friends.

Case Study: Independence

Alan Acosta, Residence Coordinator
University Housing, Florida State University

Alan Acosta said that becoming independent while maintaining family ties is something that most students, not just freshmen, struggle with throughout their time in college.

He said that students have to get to a place where they are comfortable standing up for them selves, their career path, love life, or any other area in their life in a firm yet respectful way. To do this, Acosta said that it is critical for students to know themselves and their family.

Case Study: Independence

The more that students understand themselves, he said, the more comfortable they will be asserting their independence. Although there is no easy or "right" way to get to that place mentally, it has to be a developmental process that each student goes through, he said.

If students are having difficulty, they should feel as if they can get good advice from people they trust, such as friends, other family members, or mentors. Acosta said these trusted individuals can help students with the resources they need to attain the independence they are seeking.

Eric Booth, M.A., Director of Residence Life
Reinhardt College

Eric Booth said that college freshmen should start establishing their independence by handling the college process themselves, such as situations with housing, the financial aid office, and other college offices.

Kelly R. Doel, Area Coordinator
University of Central Florida

Homesickness can be especially difficult for freshmen to deal with during their first semester in college, Kelly Doel said. If freshmen get involved on campus and meet new people, they will be able deal with living in an environment without the daily support system they are accustomed to from high school. Instead of calling parents three times a day, she advised students to limit phone calls to one per day. Eventually, the daily phone call may not be necessary. Doel said moving to college is a good opportunity for students to learn how to handle situations independently, such as visiting offices and making phone calls on their own. She also said when family members see that their student is acting independently and responsibly, they will not feel as much of a need to be in constant contact.

Ashley Chittum, Sophomore
Tennessee Wesleyan College

Ashley Chittum said her first year living on her own did not seem like a big deal to her. But a friend of hers came from an overly protective family life and then went wild when she got to college. Chittum said students from sheltered family

Case Study: Independence

lives will almost certainly always go a little crazy when they first get to college while they learn to establish balance.

Carolynn S. Nath, Area Coordinator
University of Central Florida

Carolynn Nath said most students of the millennial generation are not overly connected to their parents. For those students who struggle with gaining their independence, it is important to have a balance with this relationship. Research shows some students communicate with their family more than three times a day, according to Nath. These students do not want to handle situations that arise, and try to defer the responsibility to family members. Public universities abide by FERPA (Family Education Rights and Privacy Act), she said, which restricts parents from handling situations, unless the student signs a release waiver. Nath said parents should encourage students to handle their own issues so they can learn to manage situations. Research has shown, and Nath warned, that students who do not learn to navigate a university or handle their own situations in college are less likely to have a job on graduation and more likely to return to living at home afterward.

Frederica Anderson, Sophomore
Savannah College of Art and Design

Frederica Anderson suggested that students establish independence by not calling their parents every day and instead making positive decisions on their own.

James John, Professional Student
Georgia Highlands College

James John moved away from his family but would come back and have dinner with them one day each week. He said this gave him freedom but allowed him to still keep family ties.

Ryan Thompson, 2008 Graduate
Southern Polytechnic State University

Ryan Thompson said college freshmen can establish their own

Case Study: Independence

independence by letting the family members be a last resort as the ones to run to for advice or financial assistance. He suggested that freshmen think of alternative methods or better solutions as to how they can handle unforeseen events by themselves. He said a student's family ties will get shorter and shorter throughout the course of his or her college years.

Derek Linn, Junior
University of Arkansas

Derek Linn said that as much as families want students to stay connected, they also will want students to become independent and to learn how to work out challenges on their own. Establishing independence is one of the most important ways for college students to grow, he said. His advice is for students to keep in touch with family on a reasonable basis. Although students will define reasonable differently, a balance should be somewhere between calling home twice a day and calling twice a semester.

Study

College is more than studying — college is for learning. Studying and scholastics should top your list of things to do at college. You are not in high school anymore, so studying is different. Finals are not like those high school tests you used to take. Finals cover all the material covered over the entire semester. Professors will pull questions from textbooks, lab work, and lectures. In class, you may find yourself in a lecture room with hundreds of other students and a professor speaking into a microphone. You will have to learn to take good notes, study your notes, read complicated texts in a short amount of time, and apply all this information to real-world scenarios. Last-minute cramming does not work in the college world.

The next few chapters cover all your scholastic concerns, including picking a major, dealing with college professors, and helpful study tips.

Effective time-management skills will also be outlined. Managing your study time effectively is the key to a successful freshman year. Interviews with college professors and tutors will help give you real-world advice in dealing with your freshman year scholastics. Your education will be the most important part of college. It will also most likely be the most challenging. Do not procrastinate studying, and do not brush aside your scholastic requirements to attend parties and other social gatherings with friends.

CHAPTER 4

A Major Issue

One of the first and maybe most frequent questions you will be asked when people find out you are attending college is, "So, what is your major?" You might be confidently answering this question with something like pre-med, business, or accounting. But what if you do not know? Whether you feel absolutely sure about your choice of a major or have no idea, I have news for you: You do not have to know yet. Even if you are absolutely certain about your major, there is a high probability that you will change your mind while you are in school.

Undeclared

You can begin your college path with an undeclared major. This simply means you have not yet decided what area you will major in. Most of your first year, if not your first two years of college, will consist of general education classes anyway. These classes are your basic courses: English, college algebra, and history. The benefit of signing up for general education classes when you have an undeclared major is that you will not be wasting any time or money by taking classes that will not fulfill graduation requirements. Speaking of graduation requirements, make sure you know what your school requires for graduation. Chapter 5, "Fully Loaded: Scheduling Classes," will cover this issue more in-depth, but for now, realize that you need to know your graduation requirements yourself. Do not rely on others, or even your advisor, to tell you what you have to accomplish or what classes you will need to take for graduation. After all, the point of going to college is to graduate, right? You are the one responsible for making sure that happens.

Use your first year and maybe even your second year of school to decide on your major. Experiment with different classes. Pick subjects that interest you, and do not be afraid to try new areas and explore your options. If you find astronomy fascinating, even if you think you would never major in it, try it out. Although you may not decide to be an astronomy major, you might choose it as a minor or just pick up some quality star-gazing tips — which may come in handy for future dates. Pick classes that match your personality and interests. If you like debating, try political science. If you are always trying to figure out why people act the way they do, look into psychology or sociology. Allow yourself the freedom to explore your interests. If there is ever a time to try new things, this is the time and place to do it.

Tell your parents it is all right if you do not know what you want to major in just yet. Many students experience pressure from their family and friends to declare a major right away. They pressure you because they want the best for you. They want you to have direction and focus and also to quickly be on the path to graduation. Be sensitive about their concerns, but tell them not to worry. You are not wasting time or their money by not declaring a major. Explain to them that you will be mostly taking general education classes in your first semester and even first year of school. Tell them that you are trying to explore your options fully and that when you do decide on a major, you want to make sure it is the right decision. Not knowing and even switching your majors in the first couple years of college is perfectly normal and not harmful to your college graduation goal. If you still are undecided as a junior or senior or decide to switch your major in the last semester of school, then they need to be concerned, and so do you.

If you are still concerned that you do not know what you should major in, do not worry. There is help for you. If not knowing your major during the first year is a big problem for you (which it should not be), there is help out there for you. Most colleges have a career center. This center will help you explore options you have for different majors and more often than not will try to help you take your interests and strong subjects and translate them into a major. Check out jobs that interest you, and look to see what degree they ask for in the job posting. Search through **www.monster.com** or **www.careerbuilder.com** to find possible careers or see what jobs are available in specific areas. Ask your professors and advisors what kind of jobs you could expect to get if you major in certain areas. Most of all, take your time deciding, and make sure you are making the best decision. If you find a job that interests you, ask experts in that field what they majored in, and then ask them why. Ask them, if they could do it over, would they still choose the same major?

Make a list of majors you are considering. Write down why you think you would want to major in each of those areas. List the pros and cons of each one. Consider the following questions:

- Do you like the job options the major tends to offer?

- What is the salary range of entry-level people in the field you are considering?

- Would a graduate degree be required to make yourself marketable or earn a decent salary?

- Would you find the required classes interesting?

- Would you want to join a club with only people in that major as members?

If You Are Sure About Your Major

Maybe you are one of those students who have known since they were five years old exactly what they wanted to be when they grew up. Maybe you are certain you want to major in psychology or civil engineering; that is good to hear. The advice to load up your first year or two with general education classes still holds true. Schedule one or two classes in your major (but not more) during your first year. Realistically evaluate the classes. Do you truly like the field as much as you thought you would? Are the classes coming easily to you, or are they the hardest classes you have? Are you interested in the courses required for your major? Do not let your emotions of wanting a major get in the way of realistically evaluating whether the major is right for you.

Do not be afraid to change your mind. Your first and second year of college should be the time when you explore yourself and your interests. Even if you have been set on being a dentist your whole life, you may find that your interests have changed. Be open and honest with yourself about this possibility. If you have a change of heart, do not feel locked into the major you have declared. It is common practice to switch your major during college. (Author confession: My major changed from biology to education to communications before I graduated college.)

Case Study: Choosing a Major — or Not

Alan Acosta, Residence Coordinator
University Housing, Florida State University

When it comes to being undecided about picking a major, Alan Acosta said, "First and most important: Do not panic or think that something is wrong." Not everyone needs to know exactly what they are going to major in when they get to college.

Case Study: Choosing a Major — or Not

Acosta also suggested that students take courses from a variety of academic disciplines to see which one sparks their interest. He recommends students take courses in business, the arts (theatre, drawing, acting, singing), biological sciences, political science, English/literature, anthropology, and nutrition/exercise sciences. Sometimes, a student knows what overall area he or she wants to study but is not sure of the specific part to concentrate on (for example, a student knows he or she wants to study business but is not sure if he or she wants to concentrate on accounting, management, marketing, or finance). In those cases, Acosta refers students to an academic advisor from that department to provide further guidance.

Eric Booth, M.A., Director of Residence Life
Reinhardt College

Eric Booth suggested that students who are not sure about their major to work with a career services office. He also said students can explore their college's core curriculum to find areas of interest.

Kelly R. Doel, Area Coordinator
University of Central Florida

Kelly Doel said that the first year of college should be a year of exploration and growth for a student. Freshmen should not get stressed out about selecting a major or changing their major. Students can take general education classes in a variety of subject areas to see what interests them while still fulfilling requirements. Students can research different programs online and by visiting offices on campus. Colleges normally offer some type of career resource center where staff members can assist in directing students toward a major that may interest them.

Jay Goodman, Graduate
Pennsylvania State University

Jay Goodman is a firm believer that college freshmen should not be in school unless they have an idea of what they want to major in. He said students will

Case Study: Choosing a Major — or Not

only be distracted, lose self esteem, and confuse themselves by trying to start college without some idea of a major. Goodman recalled that his roommate and best friend his freshman year was so lost about his future that he got fed up, quit school, and joined the Navy. After his three-year stint, he went back to school and finished a management of information systems degree in two and a half years. Goodman said that by waiting, his friend avoided putting himself in debt and wasting a few years of his life trying to figure it out while in school.

Ashley Chittum, Sophomore
Tennessee Wesleyan College

Ashley Chittum had no problem picking her major. She has wanted to be a doctor since she was young and is now a pre-med major. Freshmen who are struggling with choosing a major should take all the college requirement classes and start looking into the areas that interest them the most. She said many of her classmates changed their majors after they started taking classes and developing interests in areas they had not explored before.

Carolynn S. Nath, Area Coordinator
University of Central Florida

Carolynn Nath said that students should not be afraid to take classes in areas they are passionate about, even if a job in that field will not earn much money. She said students would be surprised at the different types of jobs that use art history, marketing, zoology, or philosophy. Career centers on campus are excellent resources to help students discover passions, skills, and talents, Nath said. Another idea for the undeclared student is interdisciplinary majors. Students can focus on more than one interest and still get a degree. An advantage of this program, Nath said, is that students do not feel pressured to study one subject. Many students with advanced placement (AP) or international baccalaureate (IB) college credits choose this option. She said these students (characteristically coming in as sophomores or even juniors) should consider all options before declaring a major, because they are missing their first year (or possibly two) of college.

Case Study: Choosing a Major — or Not

She also suggested that undeclared students should consider taking courses in the summer as early enrollment. This will help them get ahead of other students coming in who know their major. Students can get acclimated to the campus and culture and also make friends before the hustle and bustle of fall semester if they choose this option.

Matthew Gramling, Sophomore
Oglethorpe College

Matthew Gramling knew long before he started college that he wanted to be a history major. Students of faith should pray about it, he said, and suggested that the students ask themselves if their area, field, or major is where God truly wants them. For those who do not share his beliefs, Gramling said they should consider what are they are best in and what are they are most interested in; these areas may not be the same. He advised students to not pick a major based on how much money they will earn in the field, because if a student picks a major based on an area they love they will be much more motivated to succeed in college and in their future career.

Frederica Anderson, Sophomore
Savannah College of Art and Design

Frederica Anderson said students should evaluate what career path they have with their desired major. She warned that waiting to pick a major can set back a student's graduation date.

James John, Professional Student
Georgia Highlands College

James John advised students to take every low-level class they can find because they never know what might pique their interest.

Ryan Thompson, 2008 Graduate
Southern Polytechnic State University

Freshmen struggling to choose a major should contemplate what they have

Case Study: Choosing a Major — or Not

a passion/enjoyment doing and see if they can major in it, according to Ryan Thompson. In addition, he said they should think about what they would not mind doing for the rest of their lives.

Derek Linn, Junior
University of Arkansas

Derek Linn's advice: Do not worry about it. There is plenty of time to work out these details. Students who are 18 years old and do not know what they want to do for the rest of their lives are not alone, Linn said. He suggested freshmen try to take a variety of basic classes and electives that might lead to some new interests.

Advisement

As a freshman in college, you will be assigned an advisor. If you are undeclared, you will most likely be assigned a general advisor. This advisor may be a professor, a member of the advisement staff, or a counselor. If you have declared a major, you should be assigned someone familiar with your major as an advisor. Depending on the size and organization of your school, your advisor may be a professor in your major area or an advisement staff member who specializes in your major.

Your advisor is your first contact to help you register for classes. He or she will help you select courses, assist you in the registering process, let you know how to add or drop classes, and even assist you in exploring majors. Your advisor should be concerned with more than just registering you for your first semester of classes. He or she should help you map out a successful course to graduation and keep helping you all the way through graduation. You might first meet your advisor at your college's orientation or might speak with him or her on the phone before you leave for school.

Get to know your advisor early, and maintain a good relationship with him or her. Ask if he or she will be your advisor for your whole four years at college or if he or she is temporarily assigned to you for your freshman year. If you know your major, ask for an advisor with experience and knowledge of your field. Your advisor may one day help you with landing internships or jobs, and so be sure to find an advisor whom you connect with and who you feel is truly interested in your success. Do not be afraid to ask questions — many of them. Plus, if you do not click with your advisor or you do not feel like your advisor knows enough about your area of interest, do not be afraid to ask to switch advisors.

Be prepared before your first meeting or talk with your advisor. Study your college's course catalog. Highlight courses that seem of interest to you. Look over your college's graduation requirements, and make sure your advisor is fully aware of the requirements as well. Although your advisor should help you make decisions about courses and be your guide to registering for classes, do not rely on him or her to know everything. As a college freshman, you will have to take responsibility for your own education, and that means making sure you get to graduation on time.

Consult unofficial advisors. Talk to older students at your school. Ask them what classes they took their freshman year of college and what they liked or disliked about them. Ask their advice on which classes are best taken early on and which ones should be saved for later years. If you have an older sibling or friend in college, even if it is not your college, ask that person for advice too. The bottom line is that you will have to make your own decisions when it comes to your college education, major, and class schedule. To make the best decisions, consult many sources and form your own opinion.

Does It Truly Matter Anyway?

The reality of life is that even if you major in biology, you might not become a biologist. English majors may end up as department managers, and psychology majors may one day be office administrators. The fact is that your major does not set anything in stone, except your graduation requirements. Be realistic and realize that in the long run you will make your own career path. Declaring a major does not lock you into a job or even a field. Many graduates will find their first career has nothing to do with their major. The point is not that you should give this no thought or pick a major randomly. The point is that you should not beat yourself up over it.

Before Classes Begin

Here is a quick list of things to not forget to take care of before you begin or even register for classes:

- **Buy a day planner:** Find a planner that you can easily carry with you to class but that has enough room to write in your class schedule, assignments, exams, and social events. Use it.

- **Take entrance exams:** I am not talking about the Scholastic Aptitude Tests (SATs) and American College Testing (ACTs) tests. Some colleges allow you to test out of college freshman courses. Look into your college's policy on testing out of subjects, and decide if you will take any.

- **Buy that book bag:** Get one now, and make sure it is a nice one.

- **Visit your college:** Take note of the closest library, computer lab, and study centers.

- **Study the course catalog:** Get familiar with the classes your college offers, and then make notes on which ones you are most interested in taking. Note that you might not get your first choice in classes because freshmen usually register last so it is important to choose a few alternatives.

- **Meet or talk to your advisor:** Make contact with your advisor early. Ask questions and be sure to mark when registration opens for classes (write it on your new day planner).

Minors and Double Majors

At some point in your college career, you may decide to pick up a minor. Some students choose a minor later on in their college experience because they happen to have almost enough classes in an area to qualify. Other students plan a minor from day one. If you are planning on having a minor, make sure you are doing it for the right reasons. A minor will not help much in your career path. Sure, you will list your minor on your résumé when you first graduate from college, but beyond that first job, you will likely never list it again. To be honest, employers are not that wowed by minors. If you do decide to pick one, make sure it is an area that you enjoy, and get a minor for that reason alone.

As for you overambitious double-major types, good luck. Double majors do not quite equal double the work, but make sure you know what you are getting into. Discuss your decision with your advisor. Chances are you will not be graduating in four years with a double major. Look at the advantages and disadvantages of having a double major. Ask yourself why you want or feel like you need a double major. How much will it help you in your career path? Are you just equally interested in two areas? Should you try to decide on one area and maybe make the other area a minor instead? Carefully look over the requirements for both majors and ask for tips from your advisors, professors, and field experts.

CHAPTER 5

Fully Loaded: Scheduling Classes

After you have considered your major options and you have met or at least talked with your advisor, you are almost ready to schedule your first classes. Notice I said "almost." You should spend much more time preparing to register for classes than registering. Most schools offer online registration, so the actual time it takes to sign up is just a few clicks of a mouse. The hard part is not the actual registering but knowing what classes to register for. Your advisor can help you with this process, but there is still a ton of work you need to do to make sure you are getting the best class schedule possible.

Course Catalog

Your college's course catalog is maybe as thick as your town's telephone book. Do not get intimidated by the size of the book (if you are already scared, just wait until you start buying textbooks). Flip through the catalog to learn how it is organized and find where the lower-level freshman classes are listed. Find your college's general education requirements. These classes are always a safe bet in your freshman year, since you will need them for any major. Find those classes and start looking through what your college offers. Look at the times they are offered and the semesters or the times of year your college offers them. Check out the prerequisites, if any, for classes you are interested in. At this point, just glance through to get familiar with what your college offers, and start thinking about what classes you would like to start your freshman year with.

Tips for Scheduling Classes

When you are ready to start creating mock schedules, which you will review with your advisor before you register, take note of the following key items:

- **Know your life style:** Are you a morning person or a night owl? If you cannot wake up before noon unless dragged out of bed by wild horses, do not schedule that 7 a.m. chemistry class. In some cases, you may get stuck with early morning or dinnertime classes, but if you have a choice, look for classes you know you will not be sleeping through every day.

- **Register early:** Register as soon as you can. Freshman-level classes can fill up quickly. Do not be stuck taking classes you did not want at times you did not want with professors you did not want, just because you procrastinated in your scheduling of classes.

- **Know your graduation requirements:** If you do not know your graduation requirements, how can you expect to graduate? That is four years away still, but do not forget that is the goal. Keep your goal in mind when scheduling your first classes.

- **Plan ahead:** Look beyond your first semester. Try scheduling for the entire year. Of course, your schedule may change, but looking ahead will help you to not miss out on classes that may be offered only at certain times of the year or have prerequisites that are offered only in the fall semester.

- **Do not overload or under-load your schedule:** It is your first year of school and your first semester at that. Do not try to take too many classes. Do not forget that you are not in high school anymore. You will need to adjust to college learning and an increase in homework and studying. Taking too many classes too soon will add more stress; you will have enough stress as it is. Conversely, do not take too few classes. Most colleges have requirements for class hours to be a full-time student. Meet that requirement the first semester, but do not try to impress anyone (including yourself) by taking more than what is required.

- **Diversify your schedule:** Mix up your classes so you are not overloaded with hard classes, with too many reading assignments, or with labs. Read the course descriptions to find out more about the classes and, if available, check out the syllabus ahead of time. If you can download course syllabi before you register, check out the due dates of major assignments and look at when finals are scheduled. Try not to schedule classes with the same exam dates; it will be overwhelming. Diversify your schedule by how hard you think the classes will be. If you are a math whiz and you know it, schedule a math class. Add to it an English class, even though you cannot write your way out of a paper bag. Schedule some comfortable classes along with ones you know will challenge you.

- **Balance:** Some students think class time is most important. For some, the professor makes the difference. Others say you should be most concerned with your level of interest in the class. So, what factor is most important in scheduling classes? The answer is all three. You should weigh all three factors and decide which one is most important to you. The answers will vary for every student. The ideal class would be one at a good time, like 2 p.m., with a professor who is both challenging and entertaining and covers a subject that you just cannot wait to learn more about. But how often is that going to happen? Chances are you will have boring professors, far too early class times and be stuck learning a subject you could not care less about. At least consider these factors so that you get classes closer to the ideal while you are registering for your tedious classes.

- **Foreign language:** Is a foreign language a graduation requirement for your college? If so, and if you took a foreign language in high school, it is a good idea to take the same language the first semester in college. Do not wait until you have forgotten all your "¿Cómo estás?" skills.

- **Take physical education (PE):** Gym was not cool in high school, but this is not high school. Colleges frequently offer some interesting PE classes, such as Tae Kwon Do and spelunking. These are not only good ways to give you a break from reading James Joyce, but they offer avenues to get exercise and meet people. With the freshman 15 looming over you, exercise will help ward off extra pounds, and it helps you cope with the stress of your chemistry class, too.

- **Take a chance:** Do not stick with just the classes you are comfortable with or that you know you will need to graduate. Of course, you want most of your classes to be those that are required, but you are not stuck to scheduling only those classes. If you are trying out different majors, pick a class in a major you think you might like, or pick one that just sounds interesting. If it is something too off the wall, you may want to ask around a bit beforehand, just to make sure you know what you are signing up for.

- **Meet your professors** before class and even before you register for classes. If you are able to visit your college before your first day of class, or if orientation occurs before class registration, try to meet the professors whose classes you are interested in taking. Tell them you are interested in signing up for their freshman scuba diving course and see what they say. If you find them boring already, you may want to consider another course instead, maybe water polo.

- **Ask older students:** If you know upperclassmen who have taken some of the classes you are interested in taking, ask them for advice. If you know they have taken a class by a professor who is teaching a class you are thinking of scheduling, ask them about the professor. Consider, though, that they are only offering their own opinions. You may disagree. You may love a professor they hated. A class someone tells you is boring may have been changed or may be taught by someone new and could be completely different than it used to be.

- **Allow time in between classes:** In high school, you took all your classes in a row, then went home and studied (maybe), and then woke up the next morning to do it all again. College is different. Classes are offered only two or three days a week. The classes are longer and require more work during and after class. Back-to-back classes can leave your head spinning in no time. Schedule your classes with good breaks in between. This break will allow you to clear your head, get in a little extra studying, or even knock out some homework while it is all still fresh in your mind.

- **Do not overload your days:** It might be tempting to schedule all your classes from Monday through Thursday and have a three-day weekend every week. It is not a good idea. Your week before Friday will be so intense that you may not be able to do anything on Friday except sleep. You will not have time to study in between classes during the week either. Opt for a schedule with Monday or Friday as a light day, but do not try to pack all your classes in a four-day week unless you have to.

- **Take freshman orientation:** I am not referring to your first-day orientation after you have moved in and your parents are still hanging around. Many colleges offer a class for freshmen. This class may be worth little or no credit, but it can provide a wealth of knowledge for freshmen. These classes help you transition into college, help you get to know your college, offer study tips, and let you meet a bunch of other freshmen all in one blow. They are by and large easy and have assignments such as writing your mission statement for college.

- **Avoid the easy A:** Do not pick classes just because you think they sound easy and you think will give you a GPA boost. Take classes to learn — that is the point of college. Easy-A classes are a waste of time (unless they happen to be part of your graduation requirements) and money. You should strive to take classes that will help you learn something and will result in a well-rounded education.

Case Study: Scheduling Classes

Alan Acosta, Residence Coordinator
University Housing, Florida State University

Alan Acosta said, first and foremost, freshmen should make sure that they are comfortable with their class schedule. Taking too many credit hours, particularly in that first term, could set freshmen up for failure because they might feel overwhelmed by the academic load required. He also said students should take at least one purely fun class each term. Also, students should consult with an academic advisor while they are finalizing their schedule. By doing this, Acosta said students will ensure they are staying on target with their academic requirements and will graduate on time. They will have to live their class schedule, and they need to enjoy it.

Eric Booth, M.A., Director of Residence Life
Reinhardt College

Eric Booth said one beneficial thing for freshmen to bear in mind when scheduling classes is to create separation. Students should schedule time off between classes so as not to feel overwhelmed or to feel as if they have to rush to get to their next class.

Kelly R. Doel, Area Coordinator
University of Central Florida

Kelly Doel stressed that college freshmen should not overload themselves when creating their course schedule. She recommended that students take 12 to 15 credits while they acclimate themselves to college-level classes. Orientation leaders can be extremely helpful to new students in suggesting classes to register for in their first semester. The first year is an excellent opportunity to take general education courses in a variety of subject areas, Doel said. She also said it is important for students to register for classes at times that they know they will attend. Students who sign up for classes at 7:30 a.m. or 7 p.m. may

Case Study: Scheduling Classes

not attend those classes regularly. In addition, she said freshmen may want to limit how many online classes they take so they can become accustomed to the full academic experience college has to offer.

Jay Goodman, Graduate
Pennsylvania State University

Jay Goodman warned that freshmen should not intentionally load up their Monday, Wednesday, Friday schedule and leave no classes on Tuesdays and Thursdays, thinking that they will have "free" days. He said this schedule will haunt students in the long run. Students can end up convincing themselves they in actuality have a free day and neglect their studies.

Ashley Chittum, Sophomore
Tennessee Wesleyan College

Unlike some students, Ashley Chittum has classes Monday through Friday. She said that with labs, there was no other option. Her normal schedule is: wake up, go to classes, eat lunch, go to classes, shower, go to work, eat dinner, study, and then go to bed.

Carolynn S. Nath, Area Coordinator
University of Central Florida

Carolynn Nath said students first must evaluate if they are morning, afternoon, or evening people. Students who like to stay up late might not make the 6 a.m., 8 a.m., or even 9 a.m. classes. If students think they will take a nap in the afternoon, they should take a morning class, have the afternoon off for a few hours, and then have late-afternoon or evening classes.

Frederica Anderson, Sophomore
Savannah College of Art and Design

Frederica Anderson said students should schedule classes only at times they know they will be up and alert for class. She said that in her first quarter, she got stuck with all evening classes, and as a morning person, she did not enjoy her schedule. Since then, Anderson has made her classes early in the day.

Case Study: Scheduling Classes

Ryan Thompson, 2008 Graduate
Southern Polytechnic State University

The best way a freshman can plan a class schedule is to produce a time-management outline, see how much study time one can include in the schedule, and then gear the study availability toward the course that would involve more in-depth study time, according to Ryan Thompson. For instance, he said, students might determine they need to have much time to study for two or three hard courses, and then maybe they can add one or two courses that would not require as much study time.

Creating a Mock Schedule

After you have glanced through your college's course catalog, know your graduation requirements, and have read through the scheduling tips, you are ready to create a mock schedule. Your advisor should help you with this step, but it is a good exercise to do before you meet with him or her. Knowing what classes you want ahead of time will only help the process flow more smoothly.

Pull out your course catalog again. Get a highlighter and start highlighting your top-pick classes. You should already have a good idea of what you are looking for in a course. Pick your top ten classes, and then rank them in order of your favorite ones. Use the course schedule worksheet in Appendix A to write in your choices. Start with your number one favorite class and write (in pencil) the class times and days this class is offered. Move through your list. When you have your top classes and their times listed on the worksheet, start arranging the classes into a weekly schedule. You may need to rearrange your schedule a few times before you get it right. After you have one mock schedule, make another. Vary the classes, class times, and days. Compare the two and pick your favorite of the two. Write the rank you gave the two class schedules on the top of the mock schedule worksheets.

Some schools offer online classes. Make sure that you check to see if the class you are registering for is an online class. Typically with online classes you do not meet in a classroom weekly and in some instances, you may never actually meet in a classroom. Correspondence with the professor and with classmates is usually done online. Students taking online classes must be highly self-motivated as they will not have a professor constantly reminding them when assignments are due. You should not be afraid to contact professors during their office hours if you have questions. Most professors of online classes make themselves available to students with questions at specific times each week. Online classes can free up time for working students, but you have to remember to stay on schedule as it is very easy to get behind in these classes.

Registering for Classes

Before you start inputting classes into your college's registration form or online application, be sure to go over your mock schedule with your advisor. Make any changes you need before you make your final selections. Ask any questions you may have about the courses or professors. Having two options for your schedule will help you easily adjust if you find your top classes have already been filled. Ask your advisor to walk you through the registration process. Ask him or her what your school's policy is on adding or dropping classes. Normally, there is time allowed to make changes to your schedule, even after your classes begin.

Preparing for Your First Day of Class

After you have registered and have a firm schedule, make a copy of it. Keep one copy with you and the other one in a safe place in case you lose the first copy. Write your schedule in your day planner, including the building and classroom number of each class for the first day. Now you have three copies of your schedule. This method may seem like overkill, but you will not want to find yourself on the first day of class without your schedule.

Tips to Prepare for First Day of Class

Here is a list of important things to do before you head to your first day:

- **Find your classes:** With your schedule in hand, visit each of your classrooms before the first day of school. You do not want to be lost on campus and late for your first class.

- **Buy your books:** When you register for your classes, you should be able to look up the required books for each class. You may be tempted to wait and buy the books after your first class; this might not be the smartest idea. For one, some college bookstores will sell out of books. If you wait too long, you may find yourself ordering your books online. Although some people find this method cheaper, you run the risk of buying the wrong version or spending a week or more without the textbook; do not start school behind the game. Having your books before class will ensure you are prepared for the homework and studying that will most certainly be assigned on the first day of class. Also, most colleges sell used books, which are books bought back by the bookstore from students. The used books are cheaper and are the first to sell out.

- **Get your pencils ready** and your pens, notebooks, and other materials. Have all your essential school supplies ready to go on the first day of class. Highlighters are also helpful.

- **Read the syllabi:** If you are attending a school that posts syllabi before the first day of school, print them out. Read through them. Look ahead to the first assignment. If you already have your books, you may be able to get a head start on some reading.

On the First Day of Class

- **Be prepared:** Have your supplies ready, your books with you, and your thinking cap on. Be prepared to learn.

- **Be excited:** Professors can tell which students are in class only because they have to be there and which students are there to learn. Come grade time, you want to be in the latter category.

- **Arrive early:** Get to class five minutes ahead of time. This rule should be applied to every class, every day. Do not be known as the guy who always shows up late. Not only will the other students notice and be distracted by your tardiness, but your professor will not like it. Again, come grade time, you will not want the professor to know you only as the late one.

- **Sit up front:** You do not have to pick a front-row seat, but do pick a seat toward the front of the classroom. Many freshman-level classes are large, maybe even hundreds of students. If you sit up front, you will have a clear view and will be more likely to pay attention, which normally means better grades.

- **Stay after class:** If you have taken the scheduling advice, you should not have to rush off to another class right away. Hang around a little late. Some professors give helpful tips or hints about upcoming tests.

- **Talk to your professor:** Introduce yourself. If you are in a class with 100 or so other students, your professor will not recall you just because you answered one question in class. Ask questions after class. E-mail your professor if he gives an e-mail address, which would normally be listed on the syllabus. Visit him during office hours, which are also listed on the syllabus.

Case Study: Being Dumb Can Be Smart When Registering

Eric Chaney, 2002 Graduate
University of Missouri-Columbia

During the second semester of Eric Chaney's freshman year, he signed up for a full load of classes, including German and geography. He quickly realized that the only German he was interested in was beer, and he logged on to the university's computerized scheduling system to drop the class before it counted against him.

Fast-forward two months, during which time he had been going to and somewhat enjoying the geography class. When he checked his grades one day, he found out that he was getting an F in German and, well, nothing in geography. He soon realized he had dropped the wrong class. He went to the registrar's office to straighten the situation out and was told that the date to drop a class with no penalty had past. So, he went back the next day and put on his best "dumb helpless freshman" act for a different employee. He still does not know if she felt sorry for him or just could not believe he did not know the difference between G-E-O and G-E-R, but she predated the transaction and dropped him out of German two months earlier.

CHAPTER 6

The College Professor: A Whole New Species of Teacher

College professors are not like high school teachers. They do not have any obligation to help you do well in their class or even pass it. Some professors will have high failure rates. They may even begin class telling you what percentage of students are likely to fail. They expect more of you and may not be as willing to help you fulfill those expectations. Some professors will be dour and may even seem downright mean. Some professors like to start out the first week of classes by appearing intimidating to weed out the disinterested students. Do not be intimidated by them. Learn to gauge each of your professors. Learn their likes, dislikes, and expectations. Treat each professor differently, because each one will be. Some professors will grade on attendance, and others will tell you they do not care if you show up or not (but do not be fooled — it is always best to attend every class).

Get to Know Each Professor

If you have not had a chance to meet your professor before class, ask around. Find out the rumors about your professors, but do not take everything you hear as fact. Rumors are not always true, as we all know, but the rumors may shed some light on your professor's personality; also visit **www.RateMyProfessors.com.** See if any other students have posted comments about a professor. Read the syllabus. Many times professors will include a brief bio about themselves on the syllabus. Even if they do not, the style of the syllabus can give insight into the professor's style and expectations.

Get on Your Professor's Good Side

I am not advising being a suck-up. Do not compliment your professor's shoes or outfit. Such tactics fail to deliver true results. You should, though, get to know what your professor likes and do your best to meet his or her expectations for you.

Tips for Getting on Your Professor's Good Side

- **Be early:** Do not show up late to class. Get there early and be ready with pen and notepad out when the professor starts class. Show your professor that you are making an honest attempt to learn as much as possible from his or her class. If you end up struggling, your effort may help you get a B — instead of a solid C.

- **Be involved in class:** Do not be a class clown or try to answer every question just to answer it. Participate in class and be genuinely interested in the class. Even if it is not the most interesting subject to you, try to be truly interested. Your professor will be able to tell if you are faking interest. Find something about the class that does interest you.

- **Pay attention:** Do not write letters home or doodle in class. Take good notes. Ask insightful questions.

- **Turn your cell phone off:** In this day and age, we always are ready to take a call or answer a text. Class time is not the time or place for this behavior. Even in a large class, it is never acceptable to answer a call. Texting during class will only distract you, even if your professor does not notice. Resist the temptation altogether by keeping your cell phone off during class. Put your phone somewhere you cannot easily get to it, and forget about it until class is over.

- **Do not ask offensive questions:** I am not talking about offensive as in, "Did you style your hair like that on purpose, or did you get your finger stuck in a light socket," although that does qualify as a question you should never ask your professor. I am referring to questions such as, "Is this going to be on the test?" This questions translates into, "I am only here to do the minimum amount of work." Professors like students who are eager to learn and are willing to work hard to gain knowledge and a good grade. Other questions to avoid include: "How much time will I have to study for this exam?" and "Will we be getting out of class early today?"

- **Be honest:** If you did not get the homework assignment done because you were out to dinner with friends, do not try to tell your professor that your computer crashed and lost only his class assignments. Lame excuses will only make your professor view you as a lazy student.

- **Ask for help:** If you are struggling with a class or an assignment, let your professor know. Do not wait until it is too late. Ask for help early, and be open to any advice. If your professor cannot give you the time or help you need, look into getting a tutor, meeting with the teacher's assistant (TA), or joining a group study session. Whatever you do, do not wait until you are failing. Let your professor know you are having trouble as soon as you realize it. Ask him what he suggests you do to get back on track, or just tell him what steps you are taking to improve.

- **Do not argue with markups or grading:** Although some professors may be open to debates on grading, most will not be. Try to learn from your mistakes and professors' markups. If you do not agree with a grade or markup, ask your professor to explain why he or she graded you that way. Be respectful. Let your professor know you want to understand what you did wrong so that you can avoid the mistake in the future. Taking this approach instead of just arguing will yield better results and keep you in good favor with your professor.

- **Do the work:** To quote Nike®, "Just do it." Do not procrastinate assignments or try and squeak by without the professor knowing that you did not complete your assignment or readings. You will only create more stress by trying to cover up the fact that you are unprepared for class, and most likely your professor will be able to tell. Plus, who are you cheating anyway? Bear in mind that you are paying a ton of money for a college education. The object is not just to get by and pass your classes. The object is to make it through with more knowledge and experience than you had before.

- **Communicate with your professor:** Visit him or her during office hours. E-mail any questions you may have. Keep the lines of communication open. You will feel more comfortable talking to him or her if you are having trouble if you have already spoken before you started struggling.

- **Go to class:** Even if your professor does not take attendance, he or she may notice if you are not there. Even if he or she does not notice you are missing, you will be missing vital information by skipping class. Many professors take test questions from their lectures. You will not know the information for the test unless you are in class. If you know ahead of time you will miss class, tell your professor. Tell him or her why you cannot make it and ask if you will need to do anything to make up the class. Ask your neighbor for a copy of his or her notes.

- **Do not "BS" your essays:** You might have gotten ⟨...⟩ bluffing in high school, but it will not work in colle⟨...⟩ professor will be reading every word of your essay. Answ⟨...⟩ questions in vague terms or over-explaining one point just to fill up space on the page will not get you extra points on the exam. Study, be prepared, and skip the BS.

Teacher's Assistants (TAs)

Teacher's assistants (TAs) are aides to the professors. They help the professors prepare for class and help research topics. TAs can also be valuable assets to students. They will have more time to answer your questions after class and often are more willing to help. Get to know your TAs if your classes have any.

Language Barriers

Many college professors are foreign. English might be their second language. Be understanding of these language barriers. Pay extra attention in class. You might have to concentrate harder to decipher the professor's accent and also to understand the information. Be patient. The more you hear your professor talk, the easier it will be to understand him or her. If you get to know your professor and meet with him or her before class, after class, or during her office hours, you will talk more than you do in class. The more you communicate with your professor, the easier it will be to understand him or her.

Case Study: Tips From A Professor

Julia Bullock, Assistant Professor
REALC (Russian and East Asian
Languages and Cultures)

Brief list of dos and do nots for the clueless

(From a professor who knows)

1. Do not address your professor as Mr. or Ms. So-and-so. Most of us have Ph.D.s and are properly addressed as "Professor" or "Dr. So-and-so." Assume this is the case unless explicitly instructed otherwise. No one will be offended if you inadvertently promote him or her. Some professors will be offended if you do not recognize their status. If they prefer to be informal, they will suggest you call them something else, but it is a good idea to begin the relationship on a more formal footing.

2. Do not begin an e-mail to your professor with "Hey." E-mails in a professional context should begin "Dear Mr./Ms. So-and-so." When addressing a Ph.D., see above. If you have gotten to know your professors well and have developed an informal relationship with them, then they may not mind, but when you initiate contact with someone you have never met before, you should follow formal conventions as a gesture of politeness.

3. Do get to know your professors, and let them get to know you. Speak up during class discussions. Ask questions. If they have regular office hours, make use of that time to get help on papers, ask for advice, or otherwise benefit from their help outside of class. It is exceedingly difficult to write a letter of recommendation for a student you have no memory of or one who failed to distinguish him or herself in any way (inside or outside of class). It is a joy to write a letter of recommendation for a student who impressed you as motivated, intelligent, and genuinely interested in the class you taught. Be that student if the professor's backing is important to you in your future plans.

Case Study: Tips From A Professor

4. Do be considerate of your professor's time. Most are terribly overworked and welcome contact with students outside of class but have to balance that against a host of other responsibilities. If regular office hours are indicated on your syllabus, then it may be fine to drop by without an appointment, but you might want to confirm with your professor that he or she is still available on the day and time you would like to stop by.

5. Do not simply walk into your professor's office outside of office hours and expect him or her to be able to drop what he or she is doing to talk with you. Make an appointment, be specific as to the nature of your query, and try not to overstay your welcome. Some professors — particularly senior professors or lecturers who are not on the *tenure track — have plenty of time on their hands and enjoy shooting the breeze with students for unspecified lengths of time. Most do not. It is not personal; they are just busy.

6. Do give your professor ample time and information to write good letters of recommendation for you, should you request one. This means informing him or her of your needs well in advance of the deadline — at least a month is ideal, but at the very least give two weeks' notice. Also, provide your professor with anything that may help him or her to write the letter — résumé, statement of purpose or other writing sample, and the name of the class you took with him or her and the semester you took it, if you are asking after the class has ended. Information about the specific program you are applying for — graduate or professional school, summer internship, or job, for example — and how it fits into your future goals would also be helpful. The more detail the professor has about you, the more specific he or she can be in the letter and the more persuasive the letter will sound to those evaluating your application.

*The status of instructors at the university level is determined by whether they are "tenure track."

Stereotypes about tenured professors who are lazy or irresponsible abound outside of academia, but for those who are subject to this system of evaluation, it is a grueling and stressful process. Professors are given a certain amount of time — six years is common — to establish their professional reputations, primarily by publishing books and scholarly articles, but also by proving themselves to

Understanding Academic Titles

Academic titles are listed here in order of ascending status. Bear in mind these are aggregate descriptions and will mostly depend on the specific conditions of employment at each school, as well as the personalities of the individuals involved. Understand these as guidelines, not rules. Finally, when building a relationship with a professor, understand that your association with him or her may continue long after the class has ended, particularly if you intend to pursue a career in his or her field of expertise. If this is the case, keep in touch even after you graduate and keep him or her apprised of your plans and aspirations. You never know when you may need to ask for advice or help in the future.

TA or GSI (graduate student instructor): These people are still in graduate school and have not yet earned a Ph.D. You do not need to call them Dr./Professor So-and-so. They may prefer you to call them by their first name. Ask if you are unsure. Normally, this person handles smaller sections of large classes under the mentorship of a professor who supervises their work. Their responsibilities vary and may include lecturing, grading papers, leading discussion sections, designing course materials, and holding office hours for additional student tutoring. By all means, develop a professional relationship with them, but do not ask graduate students for a letter of recommendation unless it is totally unavoidable. If this is the case, see if the professor can sign off on it. Sometimes, the professor will ask the graduate student to write the letter. But whenever possible, have someone with a Ph.D. sign the letter.

Lecturers/instructors are not on the tenure track and may not be teaching full-time. Most are employed on a contractual basis for a specified length of time. "Permanent" lecturers have longer, renewable contracts; temporary or guest lecturers are characteristically on a one-year or short-term, non-renewable contract. Nevertheless, most still have Ph.D.s. Assume that they do. Permanent lecturers have higher status than temporary ones and are better bets for letters of recommendation. After they leave their position at your school, it may be difficult to contact them for future assistance.

Assistant professors have a Ph.D. and are on the tenure track but do not yet have tenure. More than any other member of academia, their lives are subject to the "publish or perish" dictum (see previous section). They will frequently be harried, but because they are relatively new to teaching, they may also have much enthusiasm for their jobs, particularly early in the tenure process. It is certainly worth building a professional relationship with them, particularly because if they do get tenure, they will be influential backers of your future plans. Just be courteous of their hectic schedules.

Associate professors have a Ph.D. and tenure, which means that their position at the university is secure and there is sometimes (not always) less pressure on them to publish. On the other hand, they may carry a large part of the burden of committee and other service work. Unquestionably ask these people for letters of recommendation and seek their professional guidance, particularly if you plan a career in their field of expertise. They will likely be around for years to come and are in a good position to mentor you as you build your own career.

Full professors (often denoted simply as an unqualified "professor") have a Ph.D., tenure, and are senior scholars in their field. They may be technically "outranked" in the administrative hierarchy by persons with titles such as "department chair," "dean," and "provost," for example, but not in terms of scholarly credentials. Given their status, they may be quite busy with committee work and other service to the field, but they may also have more time for you by virtue of their established positions. On the other hand, they may be closer to retirement and may not be around to help you in a long-term sense as long as some of their more junior colleagues. Certainly get to know them, but as in all cases, be respectful of their time.

Case Study: Dealing with Professors

Alan Acosta, Residence Coordinator
University Housing, Florida State University

Dealing with professors is vastly different than dealing with high school teachers. As Alan Acosta put it, college professors do not have to be as "customer service friendly" as high school teachers do.

Although he said he believes that most professors will do everything they can to help students succeed, professors can do essentially whatever they think is right and that will be the end of the matter. He said students should feel comfortable with their professors and always encourages students to go visit their professors during office hours. Students should get to know their professors and build a positive relationship with them. Although not every professor will reciprocate the gesture of good faith, most are happy to interact with students. If a freshman has an issue with a professor, Acosta suggested that the student first talk to that professor. This method allows the professor the opportunity to explain to the student why he or she does things a certain way, which could resolve the issue quickly. If the student is not satisfied, then Acosta recommended talking to the dean of that specific college.

Eric Booth, M.A., Director of Residence Life
Reinhardt College

Eric Booth said that at small schools, there is much focus on personal attention

Case Study: Dealing with Professors

and interaction with faculty. He advised that students should set up a time to meet with their professors face to face early on in the semester so that they can build a rapport.

Kelly R. Doel, Area Coordinator
University of Central Florida

Kelly Doel said that even though college professors normally do not seek out interactions with students, they by and large are more than willing to help students if they visit during normal office hours. She said that personal interactions, as opposed to e-mails, are more effective in communicating with professors.

Students who approach professors with respect and without expecting exceptions will most likely find it an incredibly positive experience, according to Doel. She said students should not be afraid to ask for help, and professors will appreciate those students who take an active role in their education.

Jay Goodman, Graduate
Pennsylvania State University

Jay Goodman's first words to freshmen who want to know how to deal with their professors were, "Do not be a suck up." He advised that freshmen should not be those "Please, please, please" and "Can we get extra credit for..." people. He said that although it may have worked for the attractive cheerleader and student council president in high school, it will not work in college. Not only will this task yield no results, but you will get laughed at by the professor and your fellow students, he said. He advised students to be straightforward with their professors. In true college style, Goodman said that sometimes it is better for students not to ask for direct help but instead they should ask their professor how they can help themselves.

Carolynn S. Nath, Area Coordinator
University of Central Florida

Professors, instructors, and teaching assistants are often conducting research studies, writing and publishing, or may be in and out of the office presenting (on a national level) about their subject matter, Carolynn Nath said. Students need

Case Study: Dealing with Professors

to understand they may perceive a professor/instructor/teaching assistant as less approachable, but according to Nath, it is imperative to meet with them, ask questions, and keep in touch with them. She said that professors can have up to 1,000 students if not more, per semester, so students should develop a one-on-one relationship, especially if they know they will have them again or if the course is in their major. Students who plan on attending graduate school will be asked for faculty references, and she said it is wise to start early and have a faculty member see them grow from day one to year four. She suggested students take advantage of tutoring opportunities, comment on a lecture, ask questions, and sit closer to the front rather than the back. And of course, Nath said, do not skip class, and be on time.

Nath recommended that students communicate (electronically) professionally with their professors. She said students should not e-mail a professor, instructor, or teaching assistant in AOL Instant Messenger or send text messages, as this most certainly will put a student's credibility into question. This informal communication, Nath said, is disrespectful. This point is also especially important in written papers, as students will unquestionably have points or even grades lowered if they do not use proper grammar and language in assignments or on exams.

Matthew Gramling, Sophomore
Oglethorpe College

Matthew Gramling has never had any trouble getting along with his teachers, whether in high school or college. He did say that professors in college will not watch over students to make sure they get their work done, which might have been the case in high school. Another difference Gramling noticed in his college professors is that they swear much more than his high school teachers did. He also said that he does not trust everything his professors tell him. It is not that his professors lie to him, but he knows there are different opinions out there and likes to research the primary source of information for himself. Unlike some of his classmates, Gramling has not experienced any intimidating professors. Also, the professors that seem scary might be the best ones to challenge them and help them learn more from the class.

Word from the Experts: Dealing with Professors

Frederica Anderson, Sophomore
Savannah College of Art and Design

Frederica Anderson said students should figure out the likes and dislikes of each of their professors when it comes to class participation, homework, and exams. She said a big difference between high school teachers and college professors is that professors treat students like adults. Professors look for students to be more proactive in class, she said.

James Johns, Professional Student
Georgia Highlands College

James Johns said students should talk to their professors and not forget that they are people too. He said students should work with their professors, not against them.

Ryan Thompson, 2008 Graduate
Southern Polytechnic State University

College freshmen can deal with professors by understanding that professors are merely a guide and tool to learn, Ryan Thompson said. The professor is supposed to equip students with the real world knowledge and experience they will need to make it in the real world. He said professors view and treat students as adults. Professors are there to prepare students on subject matter, but it is the student's responsibility to work on and grasp the information.

Eric Chaney, 2002 Graduate
University of Missouri-Columbia

Eric Chaney said it is helpful for students to know what kind of professor they will have in any given class. Students should find out if their professor is a by-the-book person, where all his lectures can be found in the text, if class attendance and participation count, or if he gives out study guides before big exams with the test questions in essence answered. Students need to attend the first few classes and figure out the important dates on the syllabus. He also

Word from the Experts: Dealing with Professors

suggested that students ask around to find out what kind of professor they have, as chances are it will not take long to find somebody who has taken that class. Finding out about a professor's likes and dislikes will save students much time and energy so that they can focus on just what is important for the class.

CHAPTER 7

Old Study Habits Die Hard (Making the Grade)

The study habits you had (or maybe lacked) in high school may not work in college. Chances are you will have to completely change the way you study for classes and exams. In high school, many of the tests consisted mostly of memorize and recall; college is not like that. In college, you will be expected to know the facts, use critical thinking skills to analyze those facts, and apply them to different situations. In essence, an all-night cramming session will not work. You will have to study on a daily basis, even if you do not have your first exam until the end of the semester.

Good Habits Start in the Classroom

Do not expect to miss every class or sit idly by in class and ace the course. You will need to actively participate in class, take good notes, and be attentive.

Here are some tips on how to study effectively while in the classroom:

- **Sit up front:** Sitting up front has many advantages. You will less likely to doodle in your notebook or send text messages to your friends if you are seated up front. By eliminating these distractions, you will be able to focus more on the class.

- **Get to class early:** Being early will help you to be prepared for class when it starts. If you are rushing in as class is beginning, you will need a few minutes to take your seat and organize your desk. By the time you get set up, you could have already missed vital notes.

- **Take good notes:** You will soon learn that college professors are not worried about whether they are talking too fast for you to keep up with your note taking. You will have to learn to write fast. You also should learn to develop a shorthand method that works for you. Make up your own abbreviations or codes so that you can write more information with fewer pen strokes. For tips on shorthand, check out **www.CollegeBoard.com**. Do not try to write down every word your professor says. You want to pick out the most important information. Do not be so wrapped up in writing your professor's last statement exactly that you miss his next five sentences.

- **Turn off that cell phone:** Put it away somewhere. You will not be able to concentrate if your phone is going off every five minutes during class.

- **Get to know your "neighbors":** Meet the students around you. Get to know them. Compare notes with them after class to see if they picked up on something you may have missed or vice versa. If you do ever miss a class, ask them for a copy of their notes, and offer the same trade for them.

- **Bring a laptop to class (maybe):** If you have a laptop and if your professor allows laptops in class, you may decide to bring it to class. Typing your notes means neater notes. If you are not a strong typist, leave the laptop in your room. Some experts also think it is better to handwrite your notes in class and type them after class. Although this method may sound time consuming, it is a good way to study. You are reviewing your notes as you type them, which helps you retain the information better. Think about whether bringing your laptop to class would help or hurt you. If you will be tempted to play games or surf the Internet (if wireless is accessible in the classroom), do not bring it. If having a computer screen in front of you will block your view and be distracting, do not bring it.

- **Bring a digital recorder:** Some students like to bring a digital recorder for recording lectures. This is helpful if you would like to review something that the professor discussed after class. It is a good idea to ask the professor if they mind being recorded and to remember that in large lecture halls it may not be possible to record lectures due to sound issues. If for some reason you need to miss a class, it may be helpful to send your digital recorder to class with a friend so that you do not miss out on something important. Also, some professors will post MP3s online after each class so that you can listen to the lecture again. You should not, however, skip class just because lectures are posted online. You will most likely miss out on a mandatory in-class assignment or pop quiz.

- **Pay attention:** Many professors test off what they lecture in class. Often, this information will not be found in textbooks or handouts. The only way to get this information is to pay attention in class and take good notes.

- **Take breaks and switch subjects:** Sitting down for long periods of time can be painful — on your bottom and brain. Do not plan on reading for four hours straight. You are likely to get bored and stop paying attention to the text. Take a few minutes' break every 45 minutes to an hour. Get up, walk around, stretch, grab a light snack or a drink, and get back in the game. Clear your head and switch subjects when you find yourself tiring.

- **Read for content:** Make sure you understand what you are reading. If you do not understand what you are reading, go back and read it again. Try reading a hard-to-understand part out loud. Sometimes, hearing it helps it click. Make sure you are getting it. Just getting through the text without comprehending it will not help you come class discussion or test time.

Study Time

Time is a coveted thing in college. You will find you are busier than you have ever been. You will be pulled in many directions and will be forced to manage your time effectively if you hope to get everything done in the time allowed. There are only 24 hours in a day; there is no changing that fact. You cannot add more time just because you have a big assignment due or a test the next day. You will need to plan ahead and manage your time wisely. Plus, do not think you can just skip lunch or sleep to try to grab a few extra hours in the day. Your performance will suffer, and you will not be using your time as effectively as you need to be.

Schedule your study time. Schedule your free time, meal time, sleep time, and anything else you plan on doing. Essentially, schedule everything. Use your day planner to block out periods dedicated solely to studying, and make it a priority. Do not skip your study time for a night at the movies with friends. Schedule that night out, but do not let it override your studying. You will need to study throughout the semester. Even if you do not have a test the next day or even the next week, you need to study on a regular basis. Review your notes from class on a daily basis. Make sure you are staying current on all your reading assignments and other homework. Write down all your assignments in your day planner, and check them off as you accomplish them.

Schedule study time when you are most productive. If you are not a morning person, you may not want to schedule study sessions early in the day. Try to schedule your study sessions when you feel fresh. If you have a grueling day of classes every Wednesday, you may not be able to plan a long study session that day. Make your study sessions work with your personality and life style, but make them work. Do not put off study sessions just because you are not "in the mood" to study. Get yourself in the mood and do it. You will regret it later on in the semester if you put off studying.

Case Study: Studying in College and Time-Management Skills

Alan Acosta, Residence Coordinator
University Housing, Florida State University

Alan Acosta reiterated, "College is not high school." Unlike high school, students need to study and work hard to achieve academic success. Freshmen must build study time into their schedule. Although Acosta said he knows it can be easy to take the focus off academics and get involved in the more exciting aspects of college life, freshmen must not forget that they attend the institution to get a solid education.

Another important thing for freshmen to remember, according to Acosta, is that they must be able to manage their time wisely and not get over-involved in extracurricular activities. He said students must find a balance that works for them. Being involved in too many organizations means they struggle academically and also are not productive members of their chosen groups. To avoid this pitfall, Acosta said freshmen should find a few select groups to get involved in and make sure that it is quality involvement.

Case Study: Studying in College and Time-Management Skills

Acosta said incoming freshmen should be open to as many new experiences as possible. "College is a time to learn about yourself, other people, and the world around you, and as long as freshmen are open to those ideas, they will truly enjoy their collegiate experience." Acosta also said freshmen should not to let things stress them out and should learn to be flexible. Many students freak out if they do not do well on their first big test or get the perfect room in their residence hall. If freshmen learn to stay positive and do not let things get to them, they might just stay sane in college.

Eric Booth, M.A., Director of Residence Life
Reinhardt College

Eric Booth said that for a freshmen to successfully navigate through their first year of school, they should develop strong study habits early. He also said that freshmen should understand the value of respect for other students, staff, and professors. Being consistent and not procrastinating when it comes to studying is what Booth said are the best methods for college students to prepare for class and tests. He said, "Establish a system early, and stick with it through your entire academic career." Unlike high school, Booth warned that students will not be able to skip studying and still get good grades. He said students should be prepared to spend more time out of the classroom to get familiar with the material.

Finding a system of prioritizing is important. At Reinhardt College, Booth assists students by giving them a handbook/planner to help encourage strong time management and scheduling skills. Time-budgeting skills that work well for college freshmen, according to Booth, include making sure to space things out and working ahead if possible on long-term projects.

Kelly R. Doel, Area Coordinator
University of Central Florida

Kelly Doel said that freshmen need to realize that studying and preparing for classes in college is exceedingly different from high school. She said students often struggle with the transition during their first semester. The most noticeable difference is that no one is there to make sure that the student attends class

Case Study: Studying in College and Time-Management Skills

and studies. Students must motivate themselves. She recommended that students do homework and study ahead of time instead of procrastinating and pulling "all nighters." Each student is different, but distractions such as instant messenger, Facebook, and text messaging can affect focus and the ability to retain information. She also advised that teaching material to another person also helps the student understand and recall what he or she has learned.

Time management is the key to success. Although it is easy for freshmen to over-commit and get involved in too many activities, she advised that students give 100 percent effort toward a few commitments, rather than give 60 percent effort to too many. According to Doel, students should try a schedule, and if it does not work, readjust until they find one that works for them. Also, they need to admit when they need help from friends or other supporters.

By not over-committing or procrastinating, Doel said students can manage their time effectively. Prioritizing daily tasks and starting to work on assignments when they are given instead of waiting until the last minute can help students immensely. Doel stressed that students should plan for the unexpected and allow time for rest and relaxation. These things can reduce the stress felt by college freshmen who have not managed their time on their own before.

Ashley Chittum, Sophomore
Tennessee Wesleyan College

Ashley Chittum said that she found that study groups work well for her. She said that even just pairing up with one other classmate can be helpful when studying.

Matthew Gramling, Sophomore
Oglethorpe College

Matthew Gramling said he found he studied much more and wrote more papers in college than he ever did in high school. He would begin studying for exams days ahead of time. One method of studying that worked well for Gramling was creating flash cards and reading over them. He said his high

Case Study: Studying in College and Time-Management Skills

school AP classes prepared him for college, but he still finds his college work more detailed and time consuming. He admitted to using SparkNotes to study but uses them only as an aid and still looks up information in the source book. He recommended that students find a quiet place without distractions to study, such as a library study room with no windows. He said that in college, students are not just expected to memorize facts; they are expected to let the knowledge sink in and then grind it up and chew on it.

Frederica Anderson, Sophomore
Savannah College of Art and Design

Frederica Anderson said that studying in college is extremely different than studying in high school. Cramming everything in the night before might have worked in high school, she said, but it does not work in college. She advised students to take detailed notes in class and review the notes every day. She also said that whatever class students find to be the hardest should be the one to study for the longest.

James Johns, Professional Student
Georgia Highlands College

James Johns said that students first need to identify the type of studier they are. He said college is different because the professors expect students to do all the studying. In high school, teachers would spoon-feed the class the information, he said.

Johns advised that freshmen make their first few weeks party-free to allow time to adjust to their new schedule. He said students should not wait until the last moment to get things finished because students who get their projects done early will have more time to relax and play.

Ryan Thompson, 2008 Graduate
Southern Polytechnic State University

The best method of studying in college includes developing a way of reviewing the notes taken in class to retain the information outlined during the lecture,

Case Study: Studying in College and Time-Management Skills

Ryan Thompson said. In college, professors will lecture, and it is the student's responsibility to take good notes. Studying in college involves being more independent in studying methods and resources. High school was more textbook-driven, so students could read the textbooks and be prepared for an exam written from the book. College exams are geared more toward the lectures professors have held.

Thompson admitted that freshmen may have to lose sleep or make sacrifices to manage their busy schedule and get things done. He suggested that students use an organizer and create a base schedule with open slots to do additional things. He also said that freshmen should be sure to not overcommit.

Study Environment

Where you study is just as important as when and how often. If you are easily distracted, find a quiet spot to study. If you cannot concentrate in your dorm room, then do not try to study there. Dorm rooms are full of distractions such as roommates, friends stopping by, television, video games, phones, and music. Some people find the library to be a quiet place to get studying done. Others find it distracting every time someone walks by or asks the reference desk a question. Experiment with different locations and find the one that is best for you. Every student is different. Try listening to classical music while you study. Many people believe that listening to Beethoven or Bach helps students concentrate when they are studying. If it works for you, that is wonderful; if not, find something that does. Do not fool yourself into thinking you can study in bed. You will either fall asleep trying to study or train your body not to sleep when you are in bed. Either way, the outcome is not good. Choose your study spot wisely.

Where to Turn When You Are Struggling

If you find yourself falling behind in a class or you just cannot seem to understand a topic, get help. College campuses are full of resources for struggling students. Look into what tutoring services are offered. If you prefer a less-formal tutoring, ask a student in your class (preferably one who is doing well) to help you. Ask if you can meet with your professor after class or during his or her office hours to talk about the area where you are having trouble.

- **Go to the writing center.** If you are struggling with writing, ask if your campus has a writing clinic. Most colleges have a clinic staffed with volunteer students, aimed to help other students improve their writing skills. Ask them what services it offers. More often than not, the volunteers will be able to edit papers before you turn them in. Plan ahead if you are using a writing clinic. The clinic aids will need time to review your paper, so do not expect them to edit a paper for you on the same day that it is due. Give them ample time to review your paper before the deadline. If the clinic offers classes, try to schedule one. Learn what you can from any edits so that you will be able to write papers without their help later on in college.

- **Meet with your TA.** TAs will have more time available than professors. They often grade assignments, so they can give you insight as to what the professor is expecting from a paper or assignment. Be open to their advice. Do not forget that the TAs work directly with your professors. They know what the professors want, how the professors grade, and what you can do to improve your grade.

- **Take a class on speed reading.** If you are struggling with getting your reading assignments done on time, you may want to invest in a class on speed reading. If your college offers a freshman skills class, speed reading may be covered in that class. You will be expected to read technical information in a short amount of time. If you master speed reading, you will be able to get through more information faster while still understanding the content.

Case Study: Academic Help

Alan Acosta, Residence Coordinator
University Housing, Florida State University

Alan Acosta said that depending on the institution, the freshman, and what area a freshman is struggling in, most institutions offer some form of academic help. This help might be tutoring in a specific subject (such as math or English) or remedial education of some kind.

Acosta also said that students should know that most institutions also have some form of mental health counseling for students that are struggling psychologically. Some institutions will offer resources specifically to students of different races (or from other countries), because students can struggle in higher education if they are at an institution where they feel as if they are unable to have consistent, quality interactions with students, staff, and faculty that can relate to their issues.

To avoid needing academic help, Acosta said students need to realize early on that studying in college is much different from studying in high school. Many students were successful in high school by studying minimally, shortly before an exam. In college, Acosta said, that will not work. Freshmen must be prepared to put in quality time studying so that they can perform successfully. He said that although there may not be a "best method" of studying, each freshman must find the method of studying that best works for him or her. Research says that students should study at least a few days before an exam, space out their studying so that they are not trying to cram, get a good night's rest beforehand, and eat something before the exam. If a student follows these broad guidelines, Acosta said he or she will likely develop successful study habits.

Case Study: Academic Help

Eric Booth, M.A., Director of Residence Life
Reinhardt College

If a student starts struggling with classes, Eric Booth said there are academic assistance and tutors available at college. He also said some schools offer "living learning" communities where academic mentors are available in the residence halls.

Kelly R. Doel, Area Coordinator
University of Central Florida

Kelly Doel said that colleges and universities work extremely hard to retain freshmen. Administrators understand that there are many aspects to a college experience, and support is offered in many different ways. There are academic advisors specifically for freshmen, academic resource centers that teach study skills and time management, and first-year experience courses that acclimate freshmen to college. In addition, some campuses have incentive programs that encourage freshmen to attend activities on campus. Residence halls often have resident advisors or resident assistants located on each floor that plan programs to encourage community building. These student leaders are normally successful in getting freshmen residents connected on campus.

Ashley Chittum, Sophomore
Tennessee Wesleyan College

Ashley Chittum said that her college offers an academic success center that has tutors available to help students with homework. She said that students should talk to their professors if they are struggling with a certain class. At her small college, she has found that the professors are truly understanding and willing to help struggling students.

Carolynn S. Nath, Area Coordinator
University of Central Florida

Carolynn Nath said that many colleges have summer programs to assist incoming college students and also offices that can help tutor students in different courses. Many courses also have graduate teaching assistants (GTAs) or graduate assistants (GAs) who are getting their master's degree in the course

Case Study: Academic Help

field. She said the assistants often have tutoring sessions and will help students learn materials when a professor is not available. Most universities also have a grade-forgiveness policy that will permit a student to take one or two courses over (although students pay for the class again) to bring up a student's GPA, Nath suggested. If available, this program would be outlined in the academic policies. She cautioned students to consider this option carefully, because failing the same course twice could result in a double F on transcripts, which would significantly lower a student's GPA.

Frederica Anderson, Sophomore
Savannah College of Art and Design

Frederica Anderson said colleges have sessions and group meetings that offer struggling freshmen tips and advice from other students on how to deal with issues that first-year college students might face.

James Johns, Professional Student
Georgia Highlands College

James Johns said his college had a course called Freshman 1101, which he found "completely worthless." This class covered the college's history and not much more, according to Johns. He suggested that students take all the low-level classes they can stand to become a well-rounded person.

Ryan Thompson, 2008 Graduate
Southern Polytechnic State University

Programs offered to assist struggling freshmen are available in the career and counseling center, which offers a vast range of programs and workshops and offers tips on time management or even résumé building, Ryan Thompson said. He said that freshmen in need of tutorial assistance can find free tutors on campus that the school employs to assist students struggling academically. In his school, there was a place known as the Advising, Tutoring, Testing/Disabilities, International Student Center (ATTIC), which provided tutorial assistance to students that needed it.

Time Management

You will not have time to waste in college. That is not to say you will not waste time in college, but you will suffer for it if you do. Your day planner, which can either be a physical book or the planner in your cell phone, should be your best friend in college, your lifeline. Take it with you everywhere you go. It is essential to effective time management. Of course, you have to use it correctly for it to do its job. If you do not write everything — absolutely everything — in it, you might as well throw it away. Write down all your classes, assignments, study time, free time, club meetings, meals, exercise, and even sleep times.

Organize your schedule. Chances are there will be more things that you need or want to do than you will have time for. Something will have to be sacrificed. To not sacrifice the wrong area, set priorities as to what events are more important than others. Classes, study time, meals, exercise, and sleep should be high on the list. Watching TV, going to parties, and club meetings should fall lower on the list. Write down your wants as opposed to your needs. Be realistic and determine which items are needed as opposed to which items are just desired. Create a priority list and stick to it.

Buy used books. Some students feel that used books with markings, notes, and highlights in them serve as sort of instant CliffNotes. This method may work much of the time, but it is not an absolute guarantee. You do not know what kind of student had the book before you. He could have been failing the class and highlighted all the wrong items. He could have had the class with a different professor, and your professor could disagree with everything the other professor thought was important in the textbook.

Say no. I am not talking about drugs, but that is a good idea as well. Learn to say no to requests. You cannot do everything, and do not forget that. Know your personal limitations. Know when you need downtime or alone time. Just because your friends want you to hang out with them does not mean you have to. Neither does it mean that they will be upset with you if you have to say no. There will be times that they say no to you, too.

Use your downtime wisely. If you are stuck in the Laundromat washing last month's clothing, bring your homework. Study while you wait for the dryer. If you are sitting in a doctor's office waiting to turn your head and cough, bring your English literature textbook.

Friends

The people you meet in college will likely become your best and longest-lasting friends. You will bond with your classmates and roommates more than you did with your high school buddies. After all, you are living, attending classes, and hanging out in your spare time with them. The following chapters talk about dorm life, dealing with roommates, and dating. You might even end up meeting your future spouse while in college (although it should not be an objective in your college life). You are in college to learn, but you will meet people along the way whom you will cherish years after graduation.

CHAPTER 8

Dorm Life

Living in the dorms is a whole new experience. You will be relying on your friends and roommates for support. You will have your own space, albeit small, and will want to make it your own.

Decorating Your Tissue Box, or, Dorm Room

The header is a bit facetious, but have you seen the size of your dorm room yet? There is not going to be much room, but what it is for sure, is yours. Make it your own. Personalize your space. Make your dorm room your haven from the brutal classes and strange professors. Consult the packing list in the first section (and checklist in Appendix A) for what you should and should not bring to your college dorm room. You will be sharing your room with someone else, almost certainly someone you do not or barely know. You will want to make your space special to you while being respectful of the fact that you will be sharing this space with someone else.

Posters are an excellent way to dress up drab walls and make your space feel more like home. Pick posters that say something about you, mean something to you, and that you will not be embarrassed about when friends and family come to visit. College bookstores often sell posters if you do not already have some from home. Be sure to read the dorm room rules before you start tacking things to the walls. Colleges often do not allow nails or holes in the walls. Tape can tear paint off the walls. Ask your RA what is approved if you were not given a list of rules when you moved in to your dorm room.

Bring pictures from home and leave room to add pictures of your new college friends and experiences. Framed pictures can be placed on desktops and nightstands and can help you feel close to your family and friends back home. They also serve as conversation starters to visiting friends. You may also want to create a collage of pictures on the wall above your desk or around your bed. These collages frequently consist of unframed photos adhered directly to the wall, with whatever adhesive is approved for such things. When creating your collage, leave room to add pictures of your college friends.

Other keepsakes and home reminders will help keep you in touch with your family and friends. Just take note that you do not want to bring anything that has too much sentimental or replacement value. A family heirloom is most likely best left at home, although bringing a picture of it might be nice. The items you bring may get broken or even stolen, so think twice before you bring something with much value to you. A favorite coffee mug or stuffed animal are good options.

Bring shrubbery. Well, at least something green to add a bit of life to your dorm room. Cacti and other desert-type plants are always a good option. You will want something small that does not require much care. You most likely will not want to bring your plant home with you on school breaks, and there will not be anyone around to water it. Find a plant that can live a while without much care.

Do not forget that your dorm room is not a permanent home. What you bring to your dorm room in September, you will be bringing home again in June. Do not bring too much, and avoid bringing too many items that are hard to pack or transport. You may not be in the same room year after year. Packing for college is only half the battle. You will also be packing for home at the end of the school year.

Dorm Room Rules

Every college campus has different dorm room rules. Getting to know yours will help you prevent getting in trouble later on. Your RA will be a good contact for learning the dorm room rules, but most colleges will let you know them up front. Rules include forbidden appliances, quiet hours, and visitation hours. If you are attending a private religious school, expect rules — that is, no men in the ladies dorm and no alcohol allowed in the dorms, whether you are over 21 years old or not. Look over the rules when you move in, and if you have questions about the rules, ask your RA.

Speaking of your RA, get to know him or her. RAs are by and large upperclassmen who were selected because they have proven themselves responsible enough to watch over the dorm. If you follow the rules and are respectful, your RA can be a good friend. If not, you may find yourself running away every time your RA pokes his or her head around the corner. Most RAs will hold regular meetings, about once a month. Attend the meetings and find out if there are any changes to the rules or if any problems have been brought to his or her attention. If your dorm has quiet hours (which is common on college campus), a common complaint will be people not respecting the hours. Quiet hours are put into place to allow students to accomplish the all-important tasks of studying and sleeping.

Cleaning

Together, you and your new roommate need to decide how clean you would like to keep your dorm room. If you are a clean freak and your roommate is a slob, you may face some interesting discussions throughout the year. See Chapter 9 for more information on dealing with roommate issues. Whatever level of cleanliness you and your roommate are comfortable with, bear in mind that a clean dorm room will be important on some level. Your dorm room will serve as your living, sleeping, dining, and entertaining areas. You will not want to bring dates over and hear, "Yuck. How do you guys live like this?" Then, of course, there will be visits from your mom. Do not make her pass out in shame that you live in such a pigsty.

Keep basic cleaning supplies on hand. A broom, mop, sponges, dish soap, hand soap, paper towels, and all-purpose cleaner should serve well as a starting cleaning package. For good old hygiene reasons, you will want to maintain a comfortable level of cleanliness. Wash your dishes promptly after use to avoid attracting bugs and bad smells. If you share a kitchen, bathroom, or common space with roommates or hallmates, it is important to respect everyone's wishes and keep the space clean. Keep couches free to sit in. How else can you invite friends over for movie night? Do not create an obstacle course of books and dirty laundry on the floor. You will be much less likely to have visitors (other than the four-legged buggy types) if you do not have a clear floor space. Do not forget to take out the trash. No one wants to live in a smelly room. If the stench from your room is emanating into the hallways and your RA has left notes saying your neighbors are starting to complain, chances are you have left something somewhere for a little too long. One more thing to add to your cleaning supply list: air freshener. Your dorm will likely not allow candles, but keep something handy to rid your space of uninviting odors.

Laundry

Doing the laundry does not mean throwing all your clothes in one hamper, dumping the hamper in the washing machine, and coming back in an hour to move your clothes (possibly all a nice shade of pink now) into the dryer. If you have not already been doing your own laundry, you will need to learn fast. Separate your clothing by color, and at least have a load of light colors and dark colors. Start reading your clothing tags. You may need to add a load of delicates to your list. Clean out all your pockets before shoving your clothes in the washing machine because pens do not mix well with soap, water, and clothes. Make sure you load the washing machine with the right amount of clothes. Do not overload the machine, or your clothes will not get cleaned adequately. Too little clothing and you will be wasting money on laundry.

Schedule your laundry days. Try to do your laundry once a week to avoid having to wear the same outfit (and, yuck, underwear) three days in a row. Pick a non-peak time to do your laundry so that you are not waiting around for a machine or coming back to find the clothes you just washed lying on the dirty laundry room floor still soaking wet. Weekends are normally busy laundry days; try to find a weekday night to designate as your laundry night.

Dorm Activities

Get involved in your dorm's activities. Your dorm will most likely have social gatherings or clubs for dorm residents. Not only are these events fun, you will be participating with people who also live in your dorm. Getting to know your dorm-mates, not just your roommates, will add to your friend list. You will meet many different people who are all living in your same building. Knowing the people who live around you will be helpful for those nights you are looking for something to do and the times that you run out of sugar for your coffee on late-night study sessions.

Hang out in your dorm's common areas. This is another excellent way to meet the people you live with and have fun doing it. If your dorm has a day room with a TV, go there to watch the big game or see what is on. Many dorms also have a common game room area. Stop by and play a pick-up game of pool or foosball.

CHAPTER 9

Am I Rooming with an Ax Murderer?

College roommates can become your best friends or your worst enemies. Most likely as a freshman in college, you will not know your roommate. You may not even have much choice in the matter. You might be sharing a room with one other person or a suite with six other people. No matter what the living arrangement, you are sure to face highs and lows with your roommate or suitemates. You may find you have absolutely nothing in common with your new roomie, or you may instantly click and be best friends from day one until the day you leave for home in the summer. Chances are that you will at some point face some conflict with the person you find yourself living with for the next nine months. Bear in mind that conflicts are normal. Although I cannot begin to offer solutions for every situation that might arise, I will offer sound advice gathered from many sources on how to deal with the most common roommate issues.

Roommate Questionnaires

Many colleges have freshmen fill out roommate questionnaires so that they can attempt to match you up with a roommate who complements your personality type. The college will try to pair you with someone it feels will work well with you. Because the college does not know you any more than your unknown roommate does, it is important that you do not lie on the questionnaire. Do not claim to be a skydiving fanatic if you have only watched skydiving on TV. If the college does pair you up with a thrill-seeker adventure type and you are more a stay-in-bed-and-read type, you are likely to face some conflicts down the road. Do not answer the questions with how you would like to be or even how you think you will be in college. Fill out the questionnaire for the person you are right now.

After You Know Your Roommate

Try to arrange a phone conversation with your roommate before move-in day. During the conversation, discuss what items you both plan on bringing with you. Some of these items you will be able to share. You both will not need to bring a TV. You may decide that one of you will bring the TV and another will bring a DVD player. Depending on the size of your room and the furniture provided by the campus, you should also discuss who will bring the following items: couch, microwave, mini-fridge, coffeepot, and small folding table (for eating, cards, and other games). Try to split the list evenly and be willing to compromise on the items that you hoped to bring. Ask your roommate when he or she plans on arriving to campus. There often is a move-in period, during which freshmen are allowed to start moving in. You may be moving in on the first day allowed, and your new roommate may not be getting to campus for a few days to a week later.

When you arrive in the dorm room, try to wait until you both are present before you start staking claim to beds, desks, and other room territories. You may think that the first one there gets priority claim, but your roommate may disagree. Do not start out the year with a fight or disgruntled roommate. Do not forget that you have nine months to live together. If there is one bed or desk that is obviously better than the other, consider a fair way to decide who gets which one. Suggest drawing straws for the best spot. You might also consider switching halfway through the year.

Case Study: Roommates

Alan Acosta, Residence Coordinator
University Housing, Florida State University

Alan Acosta said his first piece of advice to students is to not judge a book by its cover. In the age of Facebook and MySpace, campus housing departments have seen an increase in the number of concerns (mostly from parents) where a student decides he or she does not want to live with a roommate because of something on the roommate's online profile, even before they have met.

If the housing department sends a student the roommate's contact information, Acosta said the student should talk to the roommate and get to know him or her. Roommates should start talking about as many things as possible before moving in, such as what items they will bring, what items they can share, and what they will need to live successfully in the room. Acosta also tells residents that if any problems arise, moving out of the room should be the last option. He advised students to try to talk it out with their roommate, get a housing staff member involved, and do their best to try to make it work. Going through that process will possibly resolve any conflicts in a more effective manner than moving out will. Finally, Acosta said, students need to be willing to compromise. Too many students come into the halls with a "my way or the highway" attitude that makes things difficult for all the roommates and housing staff. Students should try to see things from the other person's point of view and be ready to work with a roommate to set up the living space, according to Acosta.

Eric Booth, M.A., Director of Residence Life
Reinhardt College

Eric Booth recommended that students be up front about their expectations and life style. He said students should show as much respect as they would like in

Case Study: Roommates

return and not talk about their roommates behind their back because it will come back to them.

Kelly R. Doel, Area Coordinator
University of Central Florida

Freshmen should attempt to communicate openly with their roommates from the beginning, Kelly Doel said. Students should not forget that everyone grows up differently and brings a unique perspective with them to college. Having roommates is an excellent opportunity to learn about new cultures and traditions. She reminds students that just because you are roommates does not mean that you have to be best friends, and having mutual respect for each other will help when dealing with conflicts that may arise.

Jay Goodman, Graduate
Pennsylvania State University

Goodman never had to face roommate questionnaires. He had known his freshman roommate since the eighth grade. Although some experts advise against rooming with a best friend, it worked out well for Goodman.

Ashley Chittum, Sophomore
Tennessee Wesleyan College

Ashley Chittum lived in an all-girls dorm her freshman year of school and roomed with a girl on her volleyball team. Although they shared a common sport interest, Chittum said they were complete opposites. Despite this fact, they got along well. For her sophomore year, Chittum will not be rooming with the same girl but said they are still friends. Her suggestions to freshmen included talking to their roommates about any issues that might arise. She said students should let their roommates know up front what they like and do not like.

Carolynn S. Nath, Area Coordinator
University of Central Florida

Carolynn Nath recommended that students ask themselves how much time they plan to spend with their roommate(s). She said students should analyze whether

Case Study: Roommates

they want their roommates to be a "social outlet." Students who do not plan to socialize much with their roommates because they are focused on academics should seek out someone compatible who honestly is in same mind-set.

Parents should not fill out their student's housing applications, as that can lead to major roommate conflicts. Although parents may have good intentions when filling out a questionnaire, Nath said they might put a student down on paper as something he or she is not (i.e., a non-smoker and early riser who does not like to party). Students need to be honest and fill out the paperwork themselves.

Matthew Gramling, Sophomore
Oglethorpe College

A Protestant, Catholic, Jew, and Buddhist all rooming together. No, this is not the set up for a joke. This was Matthew Gramling's freshman year roommate experience. He said they soon were all joking about their differences and that they never had any serious conflicts. His school offers a roommate constitution, but even with this eclectic mix of backgrounds, Gramling and his roommates did not need it. He advised that students talk to their roommates about any issues that arise. If they cannot resolve the conflict at that level, they can talk to their RA, who can mediate a discussion between roommates. As a last resort, roommates can ask to move dorm rooms when issues cannot be resolved any other way. One tip he offered is for roommates not to take things from each other without asking.

Frederica Anderson, Sophomore
Savannah College of Art and Design

Frederica Anderson advised that students should respect each other and each other's privacy. She said students who have issues with their roommates should talk to save headaches in the future.

James Johns, Professional Student
Georgia Highlands College

James Johns summed up how to deal with roommate issues in one word:

Case Study: Roommates

communication. He said he spent much time being angry at someone for something so little when he should have just approached his roommate and talked with him. He also stresses that respect is key to any living scenario.

Ryan Thompson, 2008 Graduate
Southern Polytechnic State University

Freshmen will have to adjust to roommates and make sure they set agreeable rules and respect each other, Ryan Thompson said, and remember that everyone will be adjusting to the new living situation.

Getting to Know Each Other

When you both have chosen your respective areas and have moved in, you will start unpacking and decorating. Take this time to also start getting to know your roommate. Be open-minded with your roommate. You may come from two entirely different walks of life. You might at first think you have nothing in common with your roommate, but do not be quick to judge. Allow you and your roommate time to get to know each other. You might end up being surprised about how much you have in common, even if you are a country boy and your roommate is still sporting the Goth look. Bear in mind that you both applied to and were accepted into the same school, so that must mean your college thought you both were the right material for that school. Your commonalities might end there, but at least you have that.

Ask questions, but do not grill the person. You are not holding the Spanish Inquisition, and your roommate is not a criminal (at least you hope not). Find out where your roommate is from, what activities he does for fun, why he chose this college, what kind of music he likes, and if he is a morning person or night owl. Again, be open-minded if your roommate answers questions differently than you would. You are just as weird to him as he is to you. Be yourself and be honest. If you do not judge him, chances are he will not judge you either. Give yourselves time to get to know each other, and try not to force a friendship.

Set Some Ground Rules

Do not be rude about it or too assertive (like you are trying to tell him he has to live by your rules), but suggest that you both sit down and create some rules for the dorm room. Make sure you both agree on any rules you decide to implement. If there are items you are sensitive about (such as never make fun of my mom or use my toothbrush), tell your roommate; ask your roommate what his pet peeves are. What are the things he gets most upset about? What is his stance on inviting friends over? When are most of his classes? Will you need to set some quiet times for your room that are different from the dorm hall once in a while? It is best to discuss issues before they become issues. Talking about rules before anyone's feelings are hurt should help prevent problems before they happen.

Not Too Close

Do not assume your roommate is automatically your new best friend. Plus, do not cling to his or her side. Make sure you both meet other people and have experiences that do not include the other one. You will spend plenty of time together over the next nine months. If you try to attach too much too soon with your roommate, you run the risk of not meeting anyone else and getting sick of each other before you are a quarter of the way through the first semester.

Case Study: Roommates or Old Married Couple?

Jay Goodman
Penn State Graduate

About three weeks before freshman orientation week, Jay Goodman was playing playoff baseball when he got cleated tagging someone out at second base.

About a week later, he went in for reconstructive elbow surgery and came out with some prescription drugs and an immobilizer from his shoulder to his hand with a waist attachment to keep his arm from flailing around; even his pinky and ring fingers had to stay wrapped. After the swelling came down and the drugs kicked in, he started packing for college with one good arm.

Moving in was not that bad for this one-armed-bandit; there is only so much stuff you can fit in the tiny dorm rooms. One of his best friends, Jeff, who lived two blocks down the street in his hometown, was going to be his roommate. So loading up the van, driving the two hours to their new home, and unpacking went smooth for the most part.

One gimpy roommate was classic enough, but on the second night at school Jeff and Jay went to a party. Inebriated, Jeff decided it would be a grand idea to jump down a flight of steps. Thus, Jeff went home for a few days to get his knee scoped and some cartilage removed. When he came back, 709 Snyder Hall became Gimpville.

He came back the same day as move-in day for non-freshmen, so their dorm floor was finally filling up with more people. They did not know anyone, so they headed to the cafeteria for dinner by themselves. This trip soon became a pathetic comedy fest as they got to the line. Jeff was on crutches as they waddled through the line to fill their trays. Jay carried Jeff's tray to the table and then went back to gather his own. Jay could not recall what they had for dinner, but he said whatever it was required cutting. "Ever try to use a knife to cut food with one arm?" Jay asked.

He slid his tray over to Jeff, and Jeff cut his food as if he were a three-year-old. To top it all off, Jeff joked around, playing the airplane game with Jay's food.

Case Study: Roommates or Old Married Couple?

At this time, Jay noticed the eyes focused to the two of them with giggles and chuckles coming in from all 360 degrees. After putting himself in their shoes for a moment, Jay started laughing too because he knew they had to look like an old married couple helping each other out with the most minuscule tasks.

Well, it did not end there. Jeff had to carefully wrap Jay's arm with plastic wrap every time he took a shower, and Jay had the duty of waking up when Jeff did just to tie his shoes before he went to class. "Fortunately," Jay said, "it was still summer, so I could get away with T-shirts and dress myself, otherwise, that would have led to another ridiculous routine." On Labor Day weekend, both guys went back to their hometown because they both had follow-up appointments with their surgeon. They shared the same surgeon, and he squeezed them in on a Saturday because they were now out-of-towners. The doctor knew Jay and Jeff were roommates and was joking around how they most likely lived like an old married couple. Jay said, "I doubt he knew how right he was."

On a side note, after about two or three days of this cafeteria comedy routine, a group of sophomores from Jay and Jeff's floor decided they had enough chuckles and joined their table for lunch. Jay said they remained good friends throughout their years of school.

CHAPTER 10

Parties, Drinking, and Morals

College just would not be college without the parties, and no college party would be complete without few mind-altering substances — alcohol being the most popular substance of choice. As a college freshman, you will be confronted with more choices than you have ever faced in your life so far, and you will not have Mom and Dad around to hold your hand or tell you "no" every step of the way. You will have to make your own decisions about what parties you should and should not go to, how much, if any, you should drink at the party, and whether you will take part in any other substances, such as marijuana. Making decisions about how you will handle these choices before you find yourself in a situation will help you prepare for how you want to respond to the offers and help you make responsible decisions without the peer pressure affecting your choice. You should find a good balance between partying and studying — and studying should take precedence. Academics should consume much more of your time than partying should.

Not Quite Legal

Chances are that as a freshman in college, you will not be 21 years old quite yet. That means that technically by law, you are not allowed to drink. Now, I am not naive enough to believe that all freshmen will wait until their 21st birthday to take their first sip of alcohol. Many of them may have indulged in a few underage drinking parties before they even left for college. So, let us talk about underage drinking honestly. You will be faced with many situations in college where alcohol will be readily available to you despite your age. I even recall attending a college fraternity party when I was still a senior in high school. The party even had a bouncer at the door checking IDs. I got a huge black "X" on both of my hands to signal to the bartender, and everyone else, that I was not yet 21 years old. But that did not stop the bartender from serving me; it was only a formality that the fraternity went through. It did not mean I did drink that night, though I could have. Underage drinking will happen, but you will need to decide if you are going to take the risk of doing so.

Campus security and police officers in college towns are not naive either. They know underage drinking will happen, and some schools, even some towns, will be stricter in enforcing this rule than others will be. Getting arrested, cited, or fined by campus personnel for underage drinking is enough to ruin just about anyone's buzz. Know the consequences of your actions before you decide to indulge. Your dorm may also have rules about underage drinking or even any drinking in the dorms. Know the policy and the punishment before you decide to risk being caught for breaking the rules. You may be risking more than you are willing to lose for one night of fun.

Follow Beer Commercial Advice

You have seen beer commercials on TV. The end of the commercial asks patrons to "Please drink responsibly." That does not mean drink while paying the bills or act older than you are while you are getting smashed at a party. Drinking responsibly means planning ahead for how much you will drink, if at all, and arranging for transportation or a safe way home before you head out. If you attend a party within walking distance of your dorm, have a group of friends ready to stumble home with you when you leave. Recall those other commercials about how "friends do not let friends drive drunk." Listen to that advice as well. Do not let someone else get behind the wheel when you know they have had too many drinks to be driving. Plus, for those of you who are not 21 or have friends who are not 21 years old yet, there is no amount of alcohol you can consume and safely drive home. If you blow a Breathalyzer, even under the legal limit, but you are underage, you will get busted. Do not do anything in your freshman year that will go on your permanent record. A driving under the influence (DUI) charge will follow you for years to come, not to mention take a huge chunk out of your already slim wallet.

Drinking responsibly in college, despite your age, also means knowing when to stay home and when to go out; know yourself. If you do not have the self-discipline to have only a drink or two at a party and stop, and you have a final the next day or a paper you need to write, sit the party out. There will be plenty of parties in your college life. You do not have to go to every one that you get invited to. Be adult enough to select which parties you should go to, and stay home on the nights you know you have too much studying to do already.

Know your tolerance. If you have never had alcohol before, you will not know what your tolerance is. Take it slow, and do not overdo it on your first night out. Do not try to keep up with upperclassmen just to try to prove something. The only point you will prove is why you should not drink more than you can handle — and you will almost certainly come to that realization when you find yourself hugging a toilet, too sick to move. Spending the night puking is not cool, no matter how you slice it. To help a low tolerance, make sure to never drink on an empty stomach, and drink glasses of water in between glasses of alcohol. If you think you will not look cool by drinking water, put your water in the same type of cup most people are drinking out of and when people ask you what you are drinking, tell them straight vodka. Some people will blindly believe you, and others will see through your fib, but with any bit of luck, at least get a laugh from your response.

One Drink Each Hour

When it comes to drinking, the common rule of thumb is not to drink more than one drink every hour. This rate was created based on studies showing that the average person can process one ounce of alcohol every hour. One ounce of alcohol is equal to one 12-ounce glass of beer (not the jumbo mug or beer bong size), one shot, or one small glass of wine. Drinking more than one glass every hour will lead to more of a buzz, for sure, and maybe a few other unexpected twists in the evening.

One drink is equal to 12 oz. of beer, 4 oz. of table wine, or 1¼ oz. of 80-proof liquor.

The Morning After: Hangovers

Many students will overdo it at least once in their college career. Maybe you will have just completed a midterm or final and decide to hit the party scene hard. You down beer after beer and stumble back to your dorm room, crashing fully clothed. The next morning, you wake up with the sun painfully burning your eyes and your head throbbing. If you are not that experienced drinking, this may just be your first hangover. You will swear to your roommate and any other nearby witnesses that you will never drink again. Of course, they will not believe you.

After you have a hangover, you can try a few things to make it pass more quickly. Drink plenty of fluids — non-carbonated and nonalcoholic; water is the best choice. Most hangover headaches are caused from dehydration. Alcohol, though it is a liquid, is not hydrating. Some schools of thought suggest to eat burnt toast. Supposedly, the carbon from the burnt toast helps absorb the alcohol left in your system. You can also try some headache medication that works best for you. More often than not, sleeping off a hangover is quite effective, though not always a feasible solution to a college student's schedule. Plan ahead. Party on nights when you know you will not have to get up early or be active the day after the party.

The best cure for a hangover is to never get one the first place. If you drink plenty of water before, during, and after you drink alcohol, your chances of getting a hangover the next day will be significantly reduced. Drinking water in combination with not drinking too much on the whole will help you never to get a hangover. You can maintain a nice social buzz without getting sloppy drunk and still have a ton of fun. You will almost certainly save yourself from committing embarrassing acts while you are drinking as well. Those drunken times when you dance on the table (or fall off it) will stick with you long after your buzz and hangover have worn off. So, think ahead before you start boozing it up. Taking over-the-counter headache medication before you go to bed seems to help prevent hangovers for some people as well. There are other over-the-counter aids that claim to prevent hangovers as well that might be worth a try. Some swear by these prevention methods, but if you drink until you pass out, chances are you will still wake up regretting you drank as much as you did the night before.

Poisoning and Alcoholism

Alcohol is a drug, even though it is legal if you are over 21 years old; do not forget that. If you drink too much, you can get alcohol poisoning and end up in the emergency room — another unpleasant experience. Watch for signs in yourself and your friends. If someone is passed out and you cannot wake him or her up, or someone is throwing up and cannot stop, he or she may need medical attention. Do not risk serious side effects or death from alcohol poisoning because you or your friends are worried about getting in trouble.

Parties should be a fun way to blow off steam and reinvigorate yourself for more studying, exams, and the stresses of college. Alcohol should not become a constant escape from reality or daily occurrence in your college life. Just because you are young and like to have fun, it does not mean you are not at risk for developing an addiction to alcohol. Watch for signs in yourself and your friends for developing alcoholism. If you have alcoholics in your family, be especially careful not to become addicted yourself. You should not need to drink to have fun, and drinking should not become the focus of every social event. If you find yourself wanting to pre-game (drinking before you go out) for every social gathering (for example, before dinner, before going to the movies, or before every college sporting event), you might be developing an unhealthy addiction. For more information on alcoholism, check out **www.niaaa.nih.gov** or ask your college counselor or healthcare provider about the signs and symptoms of alcoholism. Do not forget that your goal during your freshman year of college is to make it to graduation.

Word from the Experts: Partying and Drinking

Alan Acosta, Residence Coordinator
University Housing, Florida State University

As with almost everything else, Alan Acosta encourages students to be safe. They should not consume alcohol if they are underage, but said that as adults, if they choose to, they need to do so in a responsible manner.

Here are a few more tips from Acosta:

1. When consuming, know your limits. He has seen too many freshmen get transported to the hospital as a result of over-consuming alcohol.

2. Do not drink alone — always make sure you are with people you know.

3. When you have a drink, make sure to guard it. There are many date-rape drugs out there, so caution is necessary.

4. Never drink and drive — always have a designated driver.

5. Despite the myths out there, alcohol does not enhance a sexual experience. Avoid sexual encounters while intoxicated — many students regret that choice.

6. There are always alternatives to drinking. Not only will this help you stay healthy, but it will help you save money too.

7. Please recognize if you have a drinking problem and find the appropriate resources if you do.

On the whole, partying, when handled responsibly, can relieve stress and be a welcome break from academics. Though, if it is abused, he said, it can have detrimental effects on a freshman's life, whether it be academically, socially, financially, or from a health standpoint.

Kelly R. Doel, Area Coordinator
University of Central Florida

Most colleges and universities post their student conduct rules online so students can easily review them before arriving to campus, Kelly Doel said.

Word from the Experts: Partying and Drinking

For students living on campus, there are normally housing rules and regulations they should be aware of in addition to university policies. Students should not forget that certain infractions of the law can affect a student's status at the college or university, even if they occur off campus. Sometimes students fail to realize that drinking alcohol underage is against the law and can result in serious consequences. Overindulging in risky behaviors on and off campus can be detrimental to the academic success of students, Doel warned.

Jay Goodman, Graduate
Pennsylvania State University

Jay Goodman said students should have fun but should not forget: "I was extremely drunk" is not an excuse for foul-ups. He said if students cannot keep themselves out of trouble when they drink, they most likely should take it easy on the booze and partying.

Ashley Chittum, Sophomore
Tennessee Wesleyan College

When it comes to parties, Ashley Chittum said students should always go out with their friends, people they trust, and also always have one person that is not drinking. She said that all freshmen will go to parties but that they should avoid any weeknight bashes.

Carolynn S. Nath, Area Coordinator
University of Central Florida

Some institutions or learning communities in residence halls may have a zero tolerance policy, Carolynn Nath cautioned. That means if students consume alcohol underage, they may be removed from campus housing or the university. Even schools without a zero tolerance policy may put students on probation (which may go on their permanent record and transcripts) for underage drinking, which could lead to suspension or removal for repetitive incidents. She said students need to read the rules and policies for campus housing. Additionally, students might have to take an alcohol assessment class, pay fines, and/or be subject to other educational sanctions, costing $50 to $500 dollars, depending on the school.

Word from the Experts: Partying and Drinking

Also, she said, if a student is arrested, then he or she has to deal with the law and possibly have a permanent record, leading to court fees and fines, alcohol counseling, and assessments. Underage drinkers might also face a phone call to a parent or guardian to come pick them up from jail, which, for out-of-state students, can mean staying overnight or a day or two in jail.

Frederica Anderson, Sophomore
Savannah College of Art and Design

Frederica Anderson said that although partying/drinking can be fun, it should not occur on campus. She warned that students caught with alcohol or loud music on campus can be written up or kicked out of the dorms.

She also said that colleges are incredibly strict about drugs on campus, and students need to be careful about who they hang out with and where they choose to party.

Beer Bellies

Besides the hangovers and risk for addiction, there is another reason for not wanting to overdo how much you drink. Alcohol is not water; it comes packed with calories as well. If you are trying to stay fit and want to attract someone, bear in mind that alcohol intake adds calories to your diet. Even light beer still has caloric rates higher than you might expect, and if you think you can drink twice as much because you are drinking light beer, think again; you might be packing on more calories than drinking full caloric beer. Beer bellies are not attractive on any sex, at any age. If you are already developing a beer belly as a freshman in college, just think of the spare tire you will have by the time you finish school. You will face enough temptation to eat fatty foods and have a big enough challenge avoiding the freshman 15 without adding more to your plate.

Alcohol is a depressant, so it not only adds calories, but it also slows down your metabolism so that you are not burning as many calories as fast as you might otherwise. Take note of that when you are drinking and deciding how often you want to drink. Maintaining a healthy life style and weight will help you cope with stress more effectively and will also help you develop healthy habits, instead of bad ones, that will stick with you throughout your adult life.

Types of Parties

There will be no lack of parties in college, and the types of parties you get invited to will be as diverse as the people you are likely to meet at those parties. Here is a list of some types of parties you might be invited to during your college experience:

- **Weeknight parties:** Parties will not be reserved for only weekends. If you are invited to a party during the week, think about what you will be missing if you go to the party. If you have an exam the next day, an early morning class, or a paper due that week, you may need to skip that party and catch a weekend one instead. On occasion, weeknight parties can be a fun way to blow off steam before Friday rolls around. Do not make weeknight parties a habit. You will end up skipping classes and missing homework assignments if you do. You may see your grades slip, which will hurt your chances for opportunities down the road and may cost you to lose any scholarships you may have been awarded.

- **Weekend parties:** A good reason to stay on campus over the weekend is to enjoy the parties offered on a Friday or Saturday night. You will be able to sleep late the next morning without worrying about skirting responsibilities, such as skipping class. Of course, your weekends will most likely be needed for some study time, paper writing, or other academic time, so do not think every weekend should be a drunk fest at night and sleep-all-day affair.

- **School-sponsored parties:** Your college will most certainly hold some school-sponsored social gatherings that will classify as parties. Depending on your school's policy, there may be alcohol at such events. These events are more often than not free, well, sort of. The student activity fee your college charges should go toward these types of events. Festivals are often held for seasons, such as fall and spring festivals. Frequently, live music and food are provided during these parties as well. Take advantage of the free or cheap parties your school holds. They often draw large and diverse crowds and are also good places to make new friends and meet people outside your normal circle of friends. Your school's larger social events, such as formal dances and homecoming, are also included in this category, although these events by and large are more expensive than the festivals mentioned earlier. Optimistically, you will want and be able to attend these more formal events as well. Homecoming will make for lifelong memories, and even if you are not the type of person who normally likes these events, you might regret missing out on them later in life.

- **Club or student organization parties:** Student clubs will often hold parties and even allow non-club members to attend. Some of these events may charge a slight fee if the club is using the event as a fund-raiser. These parties can offer a new perspective or a diverse setting that may be interesting to you. If you attend a foreign club party, you might be introduced to new foods and cultural traditions that you would not have otherwise had the chance to experience. Try to be open-minded if you receive an invitation to a specialty club's party. Just because the chess club is throwing a party does not mean it will be full of bow-tie wearing geeks that will spend all night arguing over who has the coolest pocket protector. You might be surprised at how much fun you can have at a party that you think will be completely lame, so, give it a shot. Take a chance on a party you have absolutely no expectations for and see how it goes.

- **Private parties:** Many parties will be thrown by students for whatever random reason they can think of to have a party. Sometimes, these parties will be for a certain occasion, maybe a birthday or because of a full moon. Other times, the parties will be held simply to have a party. The party might be held on or off campus. Unless the party is on campus, chances are it will be completely without rules. Even if the party is on campus and there are rules about what can and cannot take place at parties on campus, chances are those rules will be broken or at least bent. These parties also have a tendency to get wild, so precautions need to be taken to ensure your safety while at such events. If the party includes alcohol, you might be paying a cover charge to get in. Depending on how official a party or how organized the host is, underage people might be stamped to distinguish them from the 21-and-over crowd. Off-campus parties might attract attention from local police. If the party is on campus, you might get a visit from campus security or the RA. The consequences for under-age drinking on campus could be stiff. Not only can you be arrested for under-age drinking, but you could be put on academic probation or expelled from your university. Read your student code of conduct for more information on what could happen if you are caught drinking. Knowing the consequences to your actions before you go to a party may stop you from making a mistake that could ruin your academic future.

- **Theme parties:** It could be a Halloween dress-up party or Hawaiian style party in the middle of January, but theme parties will always find a way into college life. If you are attending a theme party, be sure to find out the theme before you go, and ask around about what other people are wearing. If you go all out and find yourself the only one dressed to the hilt, you may wish you had not spent the time and effort you did to prepare. Asking questions before you go will help you avoid any possible embarrassment at the party itself.

- **Greek parties:** If your college has Greek organizations, there are sure to be Greek parties. These parties may have their own set of rules, especially if you are not a member of the fraternity or sorority that is hosting the party. If you have never attended a Greek-sponsored party before, be sure to ask around about what to expect from such a party. Although some fraternities and sororities are known more for partying than others, most of these parties will be on the wild side. Know what you are getting into before you get there.

Safety at Parties

Whether the party is on or off campus, make arrangements to go with a group, and be sure to leave with the same group. Make a pact with your friends that you all will watch out for each other. If one of you drinks too much to make wise choices, and someone at the party is taking advantage of that fact (or even trying to), make sure your friends will be there to step in on their behalf; this advice holds true for both men and women. Do not go to a party alone or as a first date with someone you just met. If someone invites you to a party where you do not know many people well, ask if you can bring a few of your close friends along. Chances are your friends will thank you for the invite, and you all will be safer knowing you have people there looking out for your best interests.

Make transportation arrangements before you leave for the party. Have a designated driver and, as a backup, have the number of and cash for a local taxi that you can call in a bind. Do not get a ride home from someone you do not know or just met. Even if this person offers to take you and your friends home, politely decline. Do not put yourself or your friends in a situation that you cannot get out of if things turn bad. If it is close enough to do comfortably and you find yourself with no other option than to walk home, make sure you let someone know when you are leaving and expect to be home just in case something were to happen to you.

If you see a campus security guard that you know, ask that person for a ride back to your dorm room. If you see a campus security guard that you do not know, ask to see an ID before taking a ride, and even then, be hesitant. Unless you know the guard or at least know that you have seen him or her around campus, be wary. Impersonating a campus security guard would not be hard, and neither would creating a fake security ID. Always be vigilant of your surroundings, carry a cell phone with you, and let someone know where you are and when you expect to be home.

Drugs

Besides alcohol, you will most likely be offered or in a position to try other drugs. Perhaps the most popular of the drugs, after alcohol, is marijuana. Depending on your background up until now, you may have already tried it. Do not forget that marijuana and other drugs you may be tempted to try during your freshman year are illegal, no matter what age you are.

Getting in trouble for doing drugs could end up on your permanent record — your police record, not just your school record. More campuses also are implementing zero tolerance when it comes to drugs. You might find yourself being kicked out of school even on your first offense. Find out what your school's policy is on drug use before you make the decision to try anything. It is likely that the risk is not worth it.

Some of the drugs you might be offered or may stumble on in your college experience, besides marijuana, include ecstasy, cocaine, heroin, and Lysergic Acid Diethylamide (LSD). Athletes run the added risk of being pressured into taking steroids, which may lead to getting kicked off the team and losing a school scholarship. Even if you are not an athlete and you do not get kicked out of school for drug use, getting caught may have you losing out on other opportunities at school. You might become ineligible for work-study and study abroad programs. You might also lose non-athletic scholarships you currently have.

CHAPTER 11

Dating

Dating in college, although inevitable, may also be a quite overwhelming and even traumatic experience if you are not prepared. You are not in high school anymore. The number of potential romantic interests just grew, and it may be necessary to take extra care to avoid trouble when it comes to dating in college. You may find yourself fighting over the same man with your roommate or someone you thought was your best friend. You might even think you have a boyfriend or girlfriend until you see that someone out on a date with someone else, so be prepared and try not to take everything too seriously. You are in college, and although dating will happen, it should not be the focus of your four years. In reality, the chances of you marrying someone you meet in school are slim. So, get out there and meet new people. If something ends up developing, wonderful; if not, do not worry. You will find that special someone sooner or later, and you may have more fun if you do not settle down into a serious relationship right away.

Take it Slow

It is week one in college and you are invited to a party. You spend hours getting ready just in case tonight is the night you meet Mr. (or Miss) Right. When at the party, you start dancing with your girls or hanging out at the bar with your dudes, and lo and behold, you catch someone checking you out. You are interested; he or she is interested — and just like that, you two go back to your dorm room and become inseparable from then to eternity. Yeah, right. Although this scenario may seem absurd now, you would be surprised how quickly college dating can progress, only sometimes, the progression ends after the dorm room.

Whether you meet someone at a party or in class, take it slow and get to know him or her. Be sure you know what you are looking for in a relationship, and find out what any possible suitors may be looking for as well. Although a party may seem like a good place to meet people, it normally does not lead to a long-term relationship — nor should it. You will not get to know someone's true personality after an hour or even a few hours at a party. If there is alcohol involved, which there more often than not will be, then you will have to be careful not to make a rash decision or judge someone based solely on your one encounter.

In today's day and age, you do not even have to exchange phone numbers with someone to get to know them better post-party. Exchanging phone numbers may not even be your best option. Instead, if you are interested in someone, get his or her screen name to instant message (IM) him or her later. You can also ask the person for Facebook or MySpace information. Through IM, you can get to know someone without the pressure of making the first call. You can take your time getting to know the person before arranging a date to meet.

Girls Only

I know that in this day and age, there should not be separate rules for girls and guys. I also know that girls are just as strong and capable as guys. Having said that, there are still special situations and circumstances that girls need to watch out for that guys may not encounter. Some girls can be more emotionally driven than guys, which means girls have to be on their toes not to be the victims of their own emotions.

When it comes to dating in college, be sure to think with your head and not your heart. You will hear some real creative stories and pickup lines from guys who seem to be all too sincere. If you have just met the guy, no matter how sweet he seems, do not believe half of what he tells you. Give yourself time to get to know him. If it truly is meant to be, then there is no reason to rush. You two will have all the time in the world for hanky-panky, so do not let a guy rush you into anything. Even if you think you want it too, give yourself time to think it over. Ask yourself how much you know about the guy. Be real about what you are feeling and what you think are his true intentions.

Upperclassmen bring on a whole new set of warnings. A female freshman in college is fresh meat to an upperclassman. They may be older and seem more sophisticated. They may be able to buy alcohol, have off-campus apartments, and drive cooler cars than the freshmen guys. But before you jump into a relationship with an older student, think realistically about all the pros and cons. Because he is older and has already completed more years in college, he will be graduating long before you do, unless of course he is a complete loser, in which case, you should run away screaming anyway. Just do not forget that when he does graduate, you will still be in school. Chances are he will find a job, and most likely it will not be in the same town as your college. Another point to consider is that dating an upperclassman may distract you from getting the full freshman experience. Most likely, you will be hanging out with your older beau and not with students in your class. Although it may seem cool at first, you may look back and regret missing some unique freshman experiences later on in your college career.

Put down the bridal magazines and step out of the jewelry store. Do not rush into things or think the first guy you meet in college will be the one you marry. Even if you fall head over heels with a guy in your first year of school, bear in mind that college is a time and place to learn about yourself and what you want out of life. What you think you want now may change. Recall your life mission statement. Do not forget that no matter how certain you are of what you want now, you might change your mind; most freshmen will. Relax and enjoy dating. Do not start planning your life with someone. Keep your own goals, dreams, and desires close. Do not lose yourself in your relationship. Maintain your own identity, interests, and friends.

College girls need to remember to be safe. Just because you meet someone on campus does not mean he is a safe person. It does not even mean he goes to your school. Group dating is a good way to ensure your safety on dates where you just met someone or do not know the person well. When you do feel comfortable enough to go on a date alone, be sure to tell someone where you are going, who you are going with, and when you should be back. This may seem a bit like reporting to your parents, but it is just part of being a responsible adult. Do not end up being a missing college student because you did not want to feel like you were still living at home. You are not asking permission to go out; you are simply letting someone know your plans. Always carry a cell phone when you are out, too. If your plans change, you will be able to let someone know. And if, heaven forbid, you do end up in a bad situation, you will be able to call for help. Another safety precaution sometimes suggested is carrying mace or pepper spray. If you decide to go this route, check your college's policy on carrying such items on campus. One warning: If you are not comfortable with these items or your attacker is stronger than you, you may find your weapon being used against you. Many campuses offer some sort of self-defense class. These classes will help teach you how to avoid bad situations and get out of one safely.

Pickup lines are cheesy at best and most times easy to see through. Just do not forget that many college guys do not have your best interests at heart. They often will say just about anything to get what they want from you. There are, though, some rather disturbing pickup lines that you may not have ever heard before. These lines have reportedly been used in real life, as sad as that might be. The first line sounds innocent enough. If a guy says, "Let's go for a walk," you might think you have met a sweet, romantic man. Beware of this line. Although you might have met a sweet guy, this line has been used by many predators trying to draw you away from your friends and into a situation where you are vulnerable. This second line is a little easier to see through, but the guys will often try to convince you it is innocent. If you are ever hanging out with a guy and he asks you, "Do you like Beefeater?" run away. He is not talking about gin, and I will just leave it at that.

Of course, there are other lines you will come across and other ploys used by men to try to deceive and trick you into doing more than you want to do. Be sure to stay alert and watch out for these and other risks when dating. Watch out for your friends, and be sure there is someone (a trusted girlfriend) around to watch out for you. If you go to a party, go with a group of friends and make a pact before you go to the party that you all will leave together — and stick to it. Having good friends to watch out for you can be one of the best safety measures.

High School Sweethearts

If you head off to college with a special someone back home waiting or at another college, you will face another unique set of challenges. Long-distance relationships are not impossible, but no one will say they are easy. Think about what your long-distance relationship will mean to you, your girlfriend or boyfriend, and your college experience. Talk it over with your sweetheart and set rules for your relationship. Some people will decide to maintain a more casual relationship and will date other people. If dating others is not what you and your sweetheart want, then set up other boundaries. Consider issues such as how often you will call each other and even possible visiting schedules.

A word of caution about long-distance relationships: You may be limiting your own college experience by maintaining a relationship back home. If you are stuck in your dorm room waiting on phone calls or leaving campus every weekend to visit your girlfriend or boyfriend, you will not be getting the full college experience. You will miss out on attending countless parties and meeting tons of new and interesting friends. Some older students warn freshmen about trying to maintain a relationship back home. These students feel as if keeping your high school sweetheart means you are living in the past, and it will prevent you from getting out and meeting other people. Plus, often the high school relationship will not last anyway, so you might as well break it off before you leave for college. On the other hand, I happen to know of high school sweethearts that have survived college and are happily married to this day. Bottom line is that you have to decide what the best road is for yourself. Evaluate all the pros and cons of a long-distance relationship, and make a decision based on what you feel is the best path for you to follow.

If you do decide to keep your old flame, bear in mind that it will be challenging. You both will need to keep the lines of communication open. You will have to have established a strong trust system and be honest with each other. Find a balance between getting the full college experience and keeping a healthy relationship. There is a definite risk that you two will grow apart simply because of the distance and the difference in experiences you both will have. You should not feel guilty for enjoying yourself or getting out and meeting new people. Be sure that your sweetheart understands that just because you meet other people or are having fun without him or her, that it does not mean you do not still love and miss him or her. Plus, if the relationship does turn sour, or if you two simply grow apart, know when to call it quits. Sometimes, the worst thing you can do is drag out a dead relationship. Most of the time, this will lead to nasty breakups and may hurt much worse than calling it quits as soon as you realize it is not going anywhere.

The Meeting

If you are not holding on to an old flame and are hoping to meet someone to date in school, you will most likely need to know where to find someone. Although there are numerous places to meet people in college, some are certainly better than others. Here is a list of some of the best and worst places to meet people in college and why some are better than others:

- **Bookworm romance:** Some of the best places to meet new dates are where you are when you are doing what you are in college to do — learn. Classrooms, study groups, and bookstores can be good places to meet new people, both as friends and as possibly more than friends. Not only will you share some common bond with people you meet in these settings, you will also have time to get to know them. Libraries have long been touted as quality pickup places, but the tide is changing. Libraries might be acceptable for flirtatious looks or scoping out the open market, but they are not the best places to meet someone. Without being able to talk much and to whisper at best, you are not going to be able to get much interaction with someone else.

- **Love at first dirty sock:** Laundry rooms are excellent places to meet new people. Do not forget that you should be studying while waiting for your laundry, so technically, I could have included this location in our first category. But laundry rooms are a bit different and deserve their own bullet point. Not only can you strike up a conversation based on what type of detergent someone uses and why, you can also sneak a peek at his or her fashion sense (or lack thereof). You may also be able to judge how much of a slob a person is by the amount of laundry they are doing at once.

- **Friendly encounter:** Networking, you should learn now, is one of the best ways to get what you are looking for in life. This theory holds true for finding jobs, getting good deals, and even dating. Meeting friends will open up doors for you to meet other people; maybe even one you will end up dating. I am not referring to getting set up or blind dates, but a casual night out with a group of friends could absolutely lead to meeting someone with future dating potential.

- **Clubbing it:** Specialty organizations, such as a biking, French, or chess clubs can work well as a way to meet people. The people you will meet in these types of organizations will share a common passion with you, which means an instant conversation starter.

- **Slam-dunk:** College campuses are hardly ever short of sporting events. Larger campuses will have more of these events than smaller schools, but whatever the size of your college, be sure to check out the sporting events. You do not have to be a mega-sports fan to don a school T-shirt and get into the spirit rooting on the basketball, soccer, or even chess team. You might meet an eligible suitor on the field or in the stands. Either way, you will get out and meet new people and have fun doing it.

- **Religious experience:** If you are a churchgoer, scope out Bible study or the pews during the sermon for possible dates. If you have strong religious beliefs, you will most likely be best matched with someone who shares the same values and beliefs as you.

- **Party on:** As I have mentioned before, parties are not the best places to meet a future boyfriend or girlfriend. This being said, you do not have to rule out parties altogether as a place to meet someone. Certain caution should be taken when or if you do meet someone you are interested in while at a party. Be sure you are being realistic about the person and the chances of their being any future beyond the bedroom that night. Despite the best intentions of both people involved, parties are loud, making conversation a difficult thing.

- **Neighborly affair:** Living in dorm rooms will open up doors to meeting all sorts of people who share the same building, if not suite, with you. Although you may find yourself close to these people and attracted to some, beware of pitfalls. If you date someone who lives that close to you, think about the consequences of a breakup. You may enjoy seeing that person every day right now, but your opinion will likely change in the event of a breakup. Breakups are far too common in college. Think twice before you decide to date someone who lives too close to you.

- **Do not look:** Many people are of the belief that the best way to find someone is to stop looking. Enjoy yourself and your college experience without worrying about finding someone to date, and maybe you will end up finding your perfect match or at least your perfect match for right now. Do not forget to relax and have fun during college. Do not worry about finding your soulmate or future spouse. Make as many new friends as possible, study hard, and have fun. You will have better chances when you stop looking than if you come off as trying too hard to find someone.

Getting the First Date

Let us imagine you have found someone you are interested in, and you do not know if this person is interested in you. Here are some tips to make the best first impression:

- **Be yourself:** You want to be yourself, but you also want to make yourself as attractive as possible. Being confident in who you are will turn heads like nothing else. People will sense your confidence and will want to get to know you more just because of it. Do not confuse confidence with cockiness. An egomaniac is not attractive, and it is not the same as a confident person who is secure with him or herself.

- **Sugar and spice and everything nice:** Be friendly, smile, and be polite. You may have gotten attention in high school by being the class heckler, but chances are your semi-rude behavior will not be appreciated by your classmates or your professors. Plus, as the old adage goes, you attract more flies with honey than vinegar.

- **Honesty is the best policy:** Be honest when you talk to people, and do not try to present yourself as being something you are not. If you are trying to date a jock and you hate sports, tell him. You do not have to share all the same interests, and if he is worth dating, he will respect your honesty.

- **Diversity dating:** Be open-minded when talking to new people. You will meet some diverse people with different backgrounds and beliefs from what you hold or have even ever heard before. Do not judge too quickly and think that just because someone holds different beliefs than you do that they are a bad person or someone not worth knowing.

- **Flirtatiously fit:** Staying in shape, besides the health benefits, will add to your attractiveness — and to your own self-confidence as well. See the *Health* section of this book, and more specifically, Chapter 13.

- **Peppermints:** Breath mints do not hurt. If you have everything else going for you but suffer from a severe case of halitosis, you may find yourself with more free Friday nights than you wish to admit.

Making the Move

If you have come this far through the dating process and have found someone whom you like and whom you think may like you back, it may be time to ask for an official date. With any luck by this point, you have been making conversation with your prospective mate. If not, it is time to start a conversation. The environment in which you know this person will have much to do with how you approach. If you know the person from a class, strike up a conversation about the paper due on Monday and maybe transition into what his or her plans are for the weekend. If you met at a sporting event or regularly see the person at sporting events, ask about a favorite player or what he or she thought of the ref's last call. Perhaps the best pickup line, if you can even call it that, is the simplest thing of all. The tried and true, "Hi, how are you," seems the best and most successful line ever invented.

In a perfect world, this process is chugging right along. You have found someone you are interested in, and he or she is interested back. You strike up a conversation. Do not be afraid to ask someone out. The worst thing that can happen is that you get told no, and then you have not lost anything. If you never ask, you are not any further ahead. So, get out there and ask.

Time to move to the next step: the first date. The most important thing is to be yourself and be honest with your date. Do not pretend to be something you are not, and do not try to mold yourself to your date. Be your own person, and be proud of who you are. During the date, ask questions to get to know your date, and when he or she answers your questions, truly listen. Do not think of the next question while he or she is still answering your last question. Listen intently to what the person is saying. You will get to know him or her better and will learn faster whether you are compatible. Answer questions accurately and honestly. Do not give the answer you think your date wants to hear; give an answer that is true. Have fun on your first date, and do not feel pressured to know whether there is a future with this person in one night. Take it slow and find out who your date is and if he or she is someone you would like to be friends with or someone you would like to be more than friends with.

Dating Wrap-Up

If you have skimmed through this chapter and have not learned anything yet, at least read this part. You may think you know all there is to know about dating, but college is different than high school. You will learn more about yourself and the type of person for you during your college years. Do not be too quick to rush into a relationship. Take your time and get to know people. Do not let anyone pressure you into doing anything you are not ready to do. Speaking of which, decide ahead of time how far you are willing to go physically with someone. If you are not ready for sex, make your decision clear ahead of time. If you do decide to have sex, make sure you know the risks. The next chapter discusses this decision and risks associated with it in more detail.

Word from the Experts: Dating

Alan Acosta, Residence Coordinator
University Housing, Florida State University

Alan Acosta said that just like eating or budgeting, romantic relationships need to be healthy. If a freshman finds that he or she is consistently arguing with a significant other; if the significant other is stressing him or her out; or if the significant other is being physically, emotionally, or mentally abusive, that freshman should evaluate whether that relationship is doing more harm than good.

According to Acosta, almost every institution will have resources available for students who are in unhealthy relationships; if necessary, freshmen should seek those resources out.

Another part of healthy relationships is sexual activity, he said. If freshmen choose to be sexually active with a partner, Acosta said they should be taking the appropriate precautions to ensure safety. Most campus health centers provide free condoms for students and also free sexually transmitted disease (STD) testing. Freshmen should use these resources as appropriate.

Eric Booth, M.A., Director of Residence Life
Reinhardt College

Eric Booth cautioned that students' reputations as it pertains to dating may determine how successful their dating life is down the road. He said students should be sure to show respect in all relationships, because most college relationships do not last.

Word from the Experts: Dating

Kelly R. Doel, Area Coordinator
University of Central Florida

Kelly Doel said that it is important for students to remain open-minded to the opportunity of meeting many people in college. Some relationships may not develop into a serious commitment, but one may, Doel said. Students should do what they feel comfortable with and should not compromise their beliefs to make someone else happy. Also, it is important to balance personal relationships with the other responsibilities associated with being in college.

Jay Goodman, Graduate
Pennsylvania State University

Jay Goodman wanted all freshmen to know that it is "time to grow up." He said students need to throw their high school dating games out the window. He also is a strong advocate of the "tie on the door system," and he was not joking. Goodman said he still has nightmares about walking in on his buddy during an intimate moment. Another word of advice from Goodman: Do not shack up with your roomie's girl or guy. He said that behavior introduces so many levels of misery that students will quickly learn that the 15 minutes of pleasure was not quite worth it, considering all the other possibilities on campus.

Ashley Chittum, Sophomore
Tennessee Wesleyan College

Ashley Chittum said in her first semester that she had a boyfriend from another college. She admitted she did better in her classes that semester possibly because she stayed in her room more instead of going out with friends.

She said all the freshmen at her small college met each other at orientation. As for where to meet people, Chittum said the cafeteria is ideal, because most students eat dinner at the same time.

Carolynn S. Nath, Area Coordinator
University of Central Florida

Carolynn Nath said students should make sure they get to know a person. As

Word from the Experts: Dating

in any situation, know who you trust and when to trust them. College is not like the movies, as many people are at school to study and to do well academically. She said students attending college for the hopes and dreams of what is in the movies such as *Old School*, *Animal House*, *Road Trip*, *Legally Blonde*, *Revenge of the Nerds II*, *Son-In-Law*, or *American Pie II* need to reconsider their goals and aspirations in college.

Frederica Anderson, Sophomore
Savannah College of Art and Design

Frederica Anderson said that dating in college is good because it helps relieve stress associated with classes. She cautioned students to consider carefully who they go on dates with and to be safe about it. She said students in serious relationships need to not forget that school still comes first.

Ryan Thompson, 2008 Graduate
Southern Polytechnic State University

On the topic of dating while in college, Ryan Thompson said the most important thing to bear in mind is that school comes first.

CHAPTER 12

Risky Business: Sex

Sex is something that every college student will have to deal with on some level. You will be confronted with people wanting it from you or talking about it to you. It is best to decide before you get to college what your stance is on sex.

Playing it Safe

The only way to completely eliminate the risks from having sex, including sexually transmitted diseases (STDs) and pregnancy, is to not have sex. If you choose to abstain from sex, find friends with similar views to be a support system. When you start dating, make your decision to abstain from sex known up front. Although you may feel uncomfortable talking about it, you will ease tension from happening later on in the relationship. If your date does not respect your decision, move on. Do not let anyone pressure you into changing your beliefs.

Sexually Transmitted Diseases

Sexually transmitted diseases are not a myth. They happen to ordinary people every day of the week. These diseases are spread through sex and sexual contact — yes, even oral sex can put you at risk for disease. It is best to know as much as possible about some of the most common diseases so that you can prevent them, and if something were to happen, you will know how to recognize it and get treated. If you do develop a STD and you do not recognize it or get treated, you will be at risk for serious complications, and you may be spreading disease to someone you care about.

Some of the most common STDs are listed below:

- **Chlamydia** is caused by a bacterial infection. Symptoms include itching and discharge. Women can be asymptomatic, meaning they will not experience any symptoms of the disease. Routine STD checks for all sexually active students are recommended to guard against having this disease and not treating it. Antibiotics are used to treat the infection, but if left untreated, serious complications can occur.

- **Gonorrhea** is similar to chlamydia and is often found in conjunction with it. The symptoms and treatment are also similar to chlamydia. If you are experiencing symptoms that are associated with either of these STDs, your doctor will run tests to determine which of the STDs you have contracted and the best course of action to treat the infection.

- **Herpes:** Herpes simplex virus (HSV) has two types. HSV-1 is associated with fever blisters and cold sores, and HSV-2 is the most common cause for genital herpes. Herpes causes blister-like sores that can last six to ten days. The lesions are highly contagious and may be spread through intercourse and oral sex. There is no cure for genital herpes, but there are treatment options to help prevent outbreaks and/or to shorten the duration of the outbreak.

- **HPV and genital warts:** There are more than 70 types of Human Papillomavirus (HPV) strands that have been identified so far. Some strands cause genital warts, and other strands have been linked to cervical cancer in women. A new vaccine is out to prevent HPV, but it must be used before a woman is exposed to this virus. Women who do not have the virus are able to get the vaccine and should ask their gynecologist about whether they are eligible for receiving the vaccine. When you have HPV, there is no cure or vaccine that can be used to treat or cure the disease.

- **HIV and AIDS:** Human Immunodeficiency Virus (HIV) is the virus that leads to Acquired Immune Deficiency Syndrome (AIDS). HIV slowly attacks the body's immune system, impairing the body's ability to fight off infections, which leads to other diseases and complications. The United Nations 2004 report on AIDS reported that about 38 million people are living with HIV, about five million people become infected annually, and three million people die each year from AIDS. Many of those infected are from third-world countries, but the threat exists for all sexually active people and those who share intravenous (IV) drug needles. In fact, according to the most recent report by the Centers for Disease Control and Prevention (CDC), an estimated 4,883 young adults received a diagnosis of HIV in the United States during 2004. This number accounted for 13 percent of the total number of people diagnosed with HIV during that year. In 2004, the CDC's data also reflected 2,174 young adults were diagnosed with AIDS and 232 young adults that had previously contracted AIDS died from the disease. Since the beginning of the AIDS epidemic until 2004 when this data was collected, an estimated 40,059 young people in the United States had received a diagnosis of AIDS, and an estimated 10,129 young people with AIDS had died. HIV is transmitted through direct contact with blood and bodily fluids such as semen and vaginal secretions. Condoms are one of the best prevention methods for this virus. Blood tests are used to determine if a person is positive for HIV, but the virus itself can be dormant for up to ten years without the patient experiencing any signs or symptoms of the disease. Practice safe sex and get tested for STDs and HIV regularly to prevent from being infected.

- **Crabs, or pubic lice:** Lice (the plural of louse) found in the pubic region can be transmitted through contact with an infected person. Itching and inflammation are symptoms, and the lice can be seen by the naked eye, though they are small. The lice resemble crabs when put under a microscope — thus the name. They attach to hairs in the pubic region. Do not attempt self-treatment. Treatment is available through doctors for this type of lice.

- **Hepatitis B** virus causes harm to the liver and is transmitted through blood and body fluids. A three-series vaccine exists for this virus, though it is not routinely given out. First responders and other medical personnel are most often vaccinated because of their risk of being exposed to blood and body fluids. Chronic liver disease can result from this virus.

- **Syphilis**, a bacterial infection, is passed from person to person through direct contact with a syphilis sore. Transmission of the organism occurs during vaginal, anal, or oral sex. Pregnant women with the disease can pass it to the babies they are carrying. Syphilis *cannot* be spread by toilet seats, door knobs, swimming pools, hot tubs, bath tubs, shared clothing, or eating utensils. Three stages of the disease exist. The first stage is characterized by chancre sores. If you experience any chancre sores in the genital area, seek medical attention immediately.

The secondary stage starts with the onset of a rash, on the palms of the hands and bottoms of the feet. The rash does not itch and sometimes can go unnoticed. The third stage of syphilis is called the latent stage. During this time, the symptoms of the first two stages will not be present. This stage can last years and can cause internal damage without a person noticing any symptoms. It is important for effective treatment of this disease to seek attention early. Antibiotics can be used to treat this disease, but some neurological damage cannot be repaired if the disease is left untreated into the latent stages.

The best prevention for STDs is by practicing safe sex through the use of condoms. Practicing safe sex means that every time you have sex, with every partner, you need to be sure you are using condoms. Getting tested frequently and not having multiple sexual partners will help reduce your risk for contracting any STD. Knowing the symptoms and seeking medical attention at the first sign of any disease will also help you get through college and life without disease. Some other conditions that are not sexually transmitted, such as yeast infections and urinary tract infections, can cause symptoms similar to some STDs. Seeking medical attention early is important to receive the proper diagnosis and treatment for any disease or condition. When it comes to your sexual health, do not be too embarrassed or shy to seek help. Medical professionals are trained and experienced in dealing with these conditions and will respect your privacy during treatment.

Pregnancy

Pregnancy is a risk for people who engage in sex. Of course, there are measures you can take to minimize your risk of experiencing an unwanted pregnancy, but bear in mind that the only 100-percent effective method is to abstain from sex altogether. If you choose to have sex, here are some options for minimizing the risk of pregnancy:

- **Condoms** are effective in minimizing the risk of pregnancy and STDs, but they must be used correctly. Be sure to check the expiration dates of condoms and store them in cool, dry places — not your wallet. Be prepared for possible sexual encounters so that you do not find yourself in a position where you decide to have sex without a condom because you do not have one readily available. It takes only one time for a pregnancy to occur or a disease to be transmitted. Condoms are not 100 percent effective, and there is a chance a condom will break during use. Have backup measures in place for such times. Both men and women should be familiar with how to properly put on a condom. Maybe some of you went through sex education class where you were humiliated in front of all your classmates by putting a rubber on a banana. If you were not fortunate enough to go through such an experience, take the time to learn for yourself before your first sexual encounter. Even if used properly and without any malfunction, condoms have a margin of error. Do you recall the *Friends* episode where Rachel gets pregnant from a one-night encounter with Ross? The story is that they used a condom, did everything right, and she still got pregnant. It can happen in real life, too. The only 100-percent protection is abstinence.

- **Birth control pills:** Women may choose to take hormones, known as birth control pills, to prevent unwanted pregnancy. Although these pills, if taken as directed, are 99 percent effective, they guard only against pregnancy, not STDs, and should not be used instead of condoms as a safe-sex practice. Women should ask their doctor about whether birth control pills are a good option for them. There are side effects of the pill, but many women find it quite effective in the prevention of pregnancy.

- **Diaphragm:** Also known as a cervical cap, a diaphragm can be used in conjunction with a spermicide to block the pathway of sperm during intercourse. Although this device, especially when used with a spermicide, can be highly effective against pregnancy, it will not protect against the transmission of STDs.

- **Morning-after pill** can be used after intercourse to prevent pregnancy for those times when condoms break or you decided to have sex without one but worry the morning after (as the name suggests) that you might become pregnant. The pill, or series of pills, contains high levels of hormones to prevent a pregnancy from developing. This pill must be taken within 72 hours of intercourse and may not be available in all states. If you have a scare and feel you need the added protection of this medication, seek medical attention or visit your local Planned Parenthood clinic for advice.

- **New methods:** Newer methods of birth control are being developed. Ask your doctor about what the best options are for you if you decide to become sexually active.

Planning ahead before you begin having sex will help prevent unwanted pregnancy and disease from ever happening. If you are too embarrassed to openly talk to a healthcare professional or your partner about safe sex practices, then you should not be having sex. As a responsible adult, you need to be comfortable discussing sex and the best way to have safe sex. If you are still seeing your family doctor and are worried about word leaking out to your parents, visit your local Planned Parenthood clinic. It will maintain your privacy (as should your local physician), and you do not need your parents' permission to make an appointment. Just do not be caught with your pants down, so to speak, when it comes to sex, pregnancy, and STDs.

Date Rape

Date rape is when you are raped by someone you know. Frequently, the attacker is someone you voluntarily go out with but who does not respect your wishes not to have intercourse. Sometimes, the attacker uses force to have his or her way with the victim. Other times, the attacker uses drugs, commonly known as date-rape drugs, to take advantage of the victim without a struggle. Common date-rape drugs include Rohyphnol, GHB, ketamine (an anesthetic used by veterinarians), and gamma-Butyrolactone (GBL, an industrial solvent). These drugs often cause the victim to have memory gaps of certain times, where one may recall most of the events of the night but have time lapses where he or she cannot recall any events. To avoid being the victim of such drugs, never take a drink from a stranger or even someone you do not know well. If you leave your drink unattended for any time period, throw it out and get a new one. If the cute boy you just met at the party wants to get you a drink, go with him and get it directly from the bartender.

If you have been the victim of date rape or think you might have been, report it. Reporting the incident does not mean you have to press charges, but it will give you the option of doing so later on. Do not shower, and report to the emergency room. Do not wash, burn, or throw away the clothing you wore at the time of the incident; all this is evidence that will be needed to file the report. The emergency room is equipped for handling rape cases, whether date rape or otherwise. The doctors and nurses can treat for STDs and pregnancy and take the evidence needed. They will also provide you with sources for help in dealing with the aftermath of such a traumatic event. Do not think you are overreacting, that you deserved it, or that you should have seen it coming. There is never an excuse for date rape, and there is never a time when anyone deserves to be raped. You have the right at any time to say no. Your date needs to respect the fact that you do not want to have intercourse.

If you have been a victim and are not sure you want to report the incident, think about the consequences of reporting the event and the consequences of not reporting it. If you report it, you will have to discuss the incident in detail more than you ever would want. Not reporting the incident means an attacker got away with a crime and may continue committing the same crime to numerous other people. Yes, it will be uncomfortable to report the event. Yes, you may be criticized for making such a decision, but think of all the future victims that you stood up for by having the courage to confront your attacker.

Health

Maintaining good health is important at all times in your life, but your freshman year of college is perhaps one of the most important times in your life to concentrate on your health. You will be making habits that will stick with you long after your freshman year and almost certainly long after you graduate from college. Being the first time you have been on your own and not under the rule of your parents, you will find yourself responsible for your own health, nutrition, and fitness. Most likely, you will get sick at some point when you are at college. Mom and Dad will not be around to take care of you or tell you when you need to visit the doctor. Your roommate might step in on occasion and help take care of you, if you are lucky. Chances are you will be fending for yourself while you are sick, and you will have to know when you are too sick to go to class, need medical attention, or just need a hot bowl of chicken soup. Unless you live extremely close to home, you will not be able to run to Mom whenever you get the sniffles, and she will not be delivering you chicken soup in bed.

Staying healthy and not getting sick in the first place will be important. In the high-stress environment of college, preventing illness will be harder and more important than ever before. The next two chapters will help you know how to prevent illness, what to do when you get sick, and how to avoid the all too famous freshman 15.

CHAPTER 13

Packing It On: Healthy Advice

This chapter will give detailed advice on avoiding the possibly mythical freshman 15 and practical advice on staying healthy while in school.

The Freshman 15

The freshman 15 is the term for the 15 pounds freshmen reportedly gain in their first year of college. Whether the freshman 15 is a myth or statistically proven is still under debate, but the reality is that you will be at risk to pack on the pounds in your first year of school. You will most likely be getting most of your meals from the cafeteria, and unless you are still living at home, you will be making your own decisions about what you eat, how much you eat, and how often you eat. Making wise choices up front will not only help you avoid weight gain during your first year, but it will also establish healthy eating habits that you can carry through your entire adult life.

Eating Healthy

Cafeteria dining in college might turn out to be much different than you are used to from high school. You most likely will have more selection, and with any luck, it will be quite tasty. Most college cafeterias are unlimited buffet-style dining. There is no one scooping out your portions or telling you not to get the double order of French fries. You will have to monitor your own serving sizes and what types of food you eat from the cafeteria. Just because your school serves pizza every day does not mean you should eat it that frequently. Exercise self-restraint, and do not load up on junk food.

May schools now have fast-food restaurants on-campus. This certainly is not helpful if your goal is to eat healthy. It is usually best to avoid these fast-food stops. The cafeteria is more likely to have meals that are balanced and nutritious. Plus, if you are using a meal plan, it may be more expensive to visit fast-food restaurants. Your campus may have delis or cafes on campus where you can get a nutritious meal. Another good alternative is to buy healthy groceries for your apartment or dorm room and bring your lunch with you to your classes. Make sure to bring a healthy snack for in between classes to keep the temptation of grabbing a burger away and keep a bottle of water with you at all times to avoid the necessity of buying sugary drinks from vending machines.

If you recall learning about the food pyramid, you will get to put that knowledge to practice. You should be thinking about the basic food groups every time you enter the cafeteria or go shopping for your dorm room snack foods. Include vegetables with your proteins and grains. Try to eat fruit for dessert instead of getting ice cream or chocolate cake. If you need to refresh your memory about the food pyramid, check the walls of the cafeteria. Your school should have the food pyramid posted in clear view. If you cannot find it or would rather view it online, check out: **www.mypyramid.gov**. Be sure to cover all food groups appropriately. Do not cheat — you are only hurting yourself. You can try to argue that carrot cake is a vegetable if you want to, but that does not mean your body will not be treating it like the cake that it is.

Stay away from the fried foods, or significantly limit the amounts of them you eat. Allow yourself a few splurges, but make them the exception, not the rule. Try new foods and explore diversity in your eating. If you are at a campus that offers different ethnic-style foods, give them a try. You may be surprised at what you end up liking. College is the time to expand your horizons, and you should feel free to explore diversity in the cafeteria and also in other areas of your life.

Plan ahead for healthy meals and snacks. Dietitians recommend eating smaller meals more often rather than having two huge meals. Pack your dorm room fridge and cabinet with healthy snack foods, and avoid the temptation of the vending machine down the hall. Low-fat yogurt, low-fat popcorn, pretzels, granola bars, baby carrots, celery sticks, and fruit (fresh and dried) all make for good snacks that are easy to eat while studying or on the run in between classes. Try to keep your cafeteria meals healthy, and allow for the snack food splurges when you have a craving for something sweet or otherwise unhealthy. Buy tiny candy bars or single-serving snack foods for those times when you want to be bad, but do not eat them on a regular basis. Your schedule is likely to be irregular while you are at school, and so your meals might end up being off a regular schedule as well. Do your best to eat small, healthy meals and snacks every few hours. Eating more often keeps your metabolism up.

Speaking of metabolism, many college students become dependent on caffeine to keep them going throughout the day. With the huge market of energy drinks, it is easy for any student to become addicted to constantly drinking super-caffeinated beverages. Beware of overloading your diet with caffeine. Drinking water will help you maintain a healthy weight and may even help you lose weight. While the amount of water a person needs daily is highly individualized and the need to drink exactly 64 ounces of water a day is most likely folk wisdom, drinking a sufficient amount of water is necessary for bodily functions to occur. It is recommended that a person urinate at least four times per day and that the urine be light in coloration. During hotter summer months or during exercise, your body sweats more and you should drink more water. It is a good idea to carry a water bottle with you while you are going about your daily routine to make sure that you stay hydrated. Use the caffeinated beverages for only those times you truly need them. Many of those drinks are carbonated, which can dehydrate you. Drinking water before meals will help you feel more full earlier and help prevent overeating. If you drink too many caffeinated beverages too often, you will start building up a tolerance to the caffeine and will find you have to drink more caffeine to get the same effect as you used to get with less caffeine.

Healthy Eating on a Budget

I do not know why it is, but it seems that healthy food is always more expensive than its junk-food counterpart. When you start to tire of cafeteria food, which is bound to happen sooner or later, you may start buying food at restaurants. Buying food at restaurants when you are on a tight budget by and large means you are eating fast food. Fast food is not healthy, but it is cheap. As a college student sometimes cheap outweighs healthy. Maybe you do not have to make that decision, though. There are ways to eat healthy and cheaply at the same time.

When shopping at the grocery store for those healthy snack foods to keep in your dorm room, look for the store-brand items instead of name brands. You will save money, and most times you will not be able to notice a difference in taste. Price-compare the sizes on the boxes. Even though you will not eat a whole box of graham crackers in one sitting, you might be getting more bang for your buck if you buy the larger size rather than buying two smaller-size containers. Coupon-clipping is not just a hobby for old ladies. You may be able to buy those name brands you truly enjoy by scanning through the coupons in the paper. It is also a good idea to request coupons for your more expensive favorite foods in care packages from home, or better yet, if these favorite foods are non-perishable, request that your parents send the actual goodie in the package. Another idea for coupon-clipping to check online for coupons to your favorite stores or restaurants.

Find the deals in the neighborhood. If the pizza place down the road has a special every Monday night, be sure to schedule your pizza nights for Mondays, but that does not mean you should eat pizza every Monday. There might be a wing place that offers a cheap wing night. Schedule an outing on the cheap night. If you need to have food delivered to your dorm room for late-night study sessions, shop around for those places with the cheapest (or better yet, free) delivery charge. And eat those leftovers. Buy a meal larger than what you can eat in one sitting, and save half for lunch the next day.

Have your friends bring their own side dishes to parties. If you decide to host a party at your dorm room, do not plan on buying the food for all your friends. You might also be surprised at how much food you are stuck with at the end. That means more leftovers, so you could be making out on the deal in the long run.

Case Study: Staying Healthy on a Budget

Alan Acosta, Residence Coordinator
University Housing, Florida State University

Alan Acosta said that there are plenty of ways to stay healthy on a budget. If a freshman lives on campus, his or her residence hall will have a wide variety of social events, Acosta said. Some of these events focus on everything freshmen will need to stay healthy on a budget, including

eating well, getting exercise, counseling services to maintain mental health, and spending money wisely.

Acosta advised that if freshmen seek out these opportunities, they will be able to maintain a healthy life style without being constantly broke.

Eric Booth, M.A., Director of Residence Life
Reinhardt College

To avoid the freshman 15, Eric Booth advised that students stay physically fit by taking advantage of college resources such as fitness centers and intramural sporting activities. These activities are excellent for students on a tight budget, because many times they are free or covered in student activity fees paid along with tuition fees.

Kelly R. Doel, Area Coordinator
University of Central Florida

Although it is easy to eat fast food and unhealthy snacks, Kelly Doel said there are options for students to eat healthy. If students have a meal plan at the campus dining hall, they can choose salads instead of fried foods, drink juices instead of soda, and skip the desserts. If not, there are numerous online Web sites that offer easy, quick, and healthy recipes for students to try, even those who are just learning to cook, Doel offered. Although establishing a weekly food budget and sticking to it can be difficult, she recommended that students

Case Study: Staying Healthy on a Budget

cook with roommates. This way she said, there will not be as much wasted as opposed to preparing individual portions; also, eat leftovers instead of throwing away food.

Jay Goodman, Graduate
Pennsylvania State University

Virtually every college has a gym, intramurals program, and cafeteria, and Jay Goodman said that students should use them. Exercising is free, and healthy food is always served in the cafeteria at incredibly reasonable prices compared to a favorite pizza joint, Goodman advised.

Ashley Chittum, Sophomore
Tennessee Wesleyan College

Ashley Chittum admitted falling victim to the freshman 15 (or so) and is now going on a diet plan. Her tip to incoming students is to not go out for fast food late at night while studying. She said students should go to the cafeteria in the evening before it closes and grab a healthy snack for later, like an apple.

Carolynn S. Nath, Area Coordinator
University of Central Florida

Carolynn Nath said there are healthy options with any on-campus dining facility. Nutritionists and dietitians are often in the health or dining centers and might set up a nutrition plan for free, Nath suggested. Students should limit on ordering out to save their budget and to help them avoid the feared freshman 15. Another word of advice: Work out. Students should take exercise classes, join an intramural sport, and use the campus walking paths.

Matthew Gramling, Sophomore
Oglethorpe College

Matthew Gramling said students can save money and be healthy if they eat on campus. He said students should set a budget for food and limit the times they eat out at restaurants.

Case Study: Staying Healthy on a Budget

Frederica Anderson, Sophomore
Savannah College of Art and Design

Frederica Anderson said students can avoid the freshman 15 by taking advantage of their school's fitness facilities as much as possible.

Derek Linn
University of Arkansas

If possible, Derek Linn said, students should eat in the cafeteria. Some schools unquestionably offer better menus than others, but there students can receive a fairly balanced meal, according to Linn. His school appears to be on a positive trend toward offering a better variety of healthier food options. He also said students should make use of the gym/recreation/workout facilities that are available on campus, especially because they are most likely paying for it already with student fees.

Fad Dieting

Eating healthy is not about dieting. It is not about South Beach or Atkins or any other popular fad diets. Stay away from diets that promise huge weight loss in extremely short amounts of time. Dropping weight fast is not healthy and often leads to regaining it just as quickly as you lost it. Rapid weight loss due to not eating or eating an unhealthy diet is dangerous because you are often depriving your body of necessary nutrients that it needs in order to perform everyday functions. Weight loss drugs can also be unhealthy because many have ingredients, such as large amounts of caffeine, that make your body behave in unexpected ways. The best and healthiest way to lose weight is to exercise and eat a healthy, balanced diet. Be sensible and keep a diet that you can stick to long term. If you have nutritionists on campus, ask them for advice on eating properly.

Carbohydrates (carbs) are not your enemy. Yes, you do not want a diet too high in carbs. You also do not want a diet too high in fat or protein. Balance your diet between the major food groups. Look at the total fat content and percentage of fat in food and also the calories of foods. If you want to know the real secret to weight loss, it is much easier than people are trying to make it. If you consume fewer calories than you burn in a day, you will drop pounds. If you take in more calories than you can burn in a day, you will gain weight. You obtain calories from food and drinks, and you burn calories from exercise. To maintain a healthy weight and life style, you have to exercise.

Exercise

Whether you are an exercise buff or a couch potato, you will want to make an effort in college to maintain a regular workout schedule. Your college will most likely have a gym you can use free of charge. Make it your goal to visit the gym three to five times a week, and vary your workout so you do not get bored and stop going. Do not overdo your workouts. Infrequent intense workouts may do more harm than good. Keeping a regular schedule of moderate exercise is the best way to get fit and stay healthy. This type of exercise will help you look your best, maintain a healthy weight (excellent for getting dates), and help reduce your stress.

Focus more on cardio when you are crunched for time, which will be more often than not. Weightlifting is good, but if your goal is to lose weight or reduce your total body weight, cardio is the way to go. Muscle weighs more than fat, and so if you are building muscle and the number on the scale is rising, do not worry. Concentrate on reducing body fat instead of lowering the number on scale. Aim for an ideal pant size instead of setting a goal weight. If your school's fitness center offers classes or counseling, take advantage of the programs. If it has a device available to measure body fat, get tested and use your ideal body fat percentage as a goal.

Ask for help from the fitness center staff. If you are not familiar with the gym equipment or you walk into the gym and feel lost, ask if someone can help you develop a personal workout system. When you get started, you will find it easier to maintain a routine. Find a few different pieces of equipment that you feel comfortable on, and vary your workout between them. Load your MP3 player with your favorite workout tunes, and jam out while you burn calories. If your gym offers aerobic or kick boxing classes, try to work a class into your schedule once a week or every so often to keep you routine varied enough to maintain your interest.

Find a workout partner. If you know someone with a similar schedule as yours, team up to go to the gym. You can encourage each other when one of you does not feel like going. Hold each other accountable for maintaining a workout schedule and keeping up with a healthy diet. Make going to the gym a fun experience. Tell yourself you cannot go see that movie you were planning on seeing with friends unless you go the gym first. Find ways to motivate yourself and your workout partner so that you are encouraged to keep with your schedule. Avoid using food as a reward, though. Telling yourself you can eat ice cream every day you work out will defeat the purpose of working out and set you on a path of bad habits, not good ones.

If working out is not your thing, and if you just cannot seem to fit in at a gym, find other ways to get exercise routinely. If your campus is bike friendly, start biking to class. Ride your bike to the store or your friend's house instead of driving or taking public transportation. Time yourself when biking to your favorite locations, and try to beat your best time. If biking is not feasible, try power-walking to class. Find a form of exercise that is both effective and fun. If you like sports but are not college-sport caliber, find a recreational team. You do not have to be like David Beckham to play soccer on a recreational league. Just make sure the team you join is still athletic. Steer clear of teams that focus on drinking during games or have to go out to the bar after every game. If you like the outdoors, find a hiking group you can join.

Avoiding Illness

Before you enter college, you are required to have certain vaccinations. Those vaccinations are required for reasons. College dorms are close living conditions and an ideal setting for diseases to spread. Colds, flu, and more serious illnesses can spread easily from dorm room to dorm room. Knowing what illnesses to watch out for and how to protect yourself from contracting these diseases will help you prevent yourself from being a victim of a college dormitory illness.

If your college does not require the meningococcal meningitis vaccination, get it anyway. This illness can be serious and has a quick onset. Meningococcal meningitis causes death in 40 to 50 percent of cases, and its symptoms can easily be confused with the flu. The close living conditions of dorms make college campuses an ideal host for epidemics of this disease. The good news is there is an effective vaccine available to prevent this illness. For around $75, the vaccine protects against the bacterial meningitis infection. A viral form of this disease can also be contracted and is not protected against with the vaccine. The viral form is less severe and often requires little or no treatment for the patient.

Women should also consider having the HPV vaccine. This vaccination is described in the chapter on STDs and should be received by women before they are exposed to the disease — preferably before they are sexually active. Ask your doctor to see if you are a good candidate for this vaccine. Some doctors are vaccinating girls before they are teenagers, so do not waste any time before finding out about this vaccination.

The flu vaccination is another one that all students should consider. Ask you doctor or college clinic whether you are a good candidate for this vaccine. Although the vaccine cannot protect against all strands of the flu, it will offer added protection against this nasty bug.

Of course, you will be exposed to other diseases that do not have vaccines available. The common cold is likely to circulate your dormitory at some time or another. To avoid catching the latest dorm room bug, take care of yourself all year long. Wash your hands with soap and water often. Antibacterial hand sanitizers should be used only in situations where soap and water are not available. There is no better substitute for good hand-washing practices, and there is no better way to prevent the spread of illness. Always wash your hands before you eat. Other ways to stay healthy include not smoking, maintaining a healthy diet and exercise program, and reducing your stress.

Relaxation techniques are an excellent help in reducing your total stress levels, especially when faced with such trying situations as you will have in college. Find a relaxation technique that works for you. Some people may find deep breathing or meditation best. A yoga or tai chi class might also work well. Maybe you just need 15 minutes alone in the park to regroup, or maybe curling up with a favorite novel is the cure for all your stress. Whatever your method for relieving stress, make sure you have one and you use it. Stress and college go hand in hand. Also, stress weakens your immune system, making it harder for your body to fight off disease. Reducing your stress will give your body an extra boost to fight off those dorm room cooties.

CHAPTER 14

Sneezes, Sniffles, and Coughs

No matter how many precautions you take against getting sick, you may end up catching something while you are in college. With any bit of luck, it will be nothing more than a common cold or stomach virus that passes quickly. When faced with an illness for the first time away from home, you almost certainly will find yourself wishing someone were around to take care of you. Do not forget that there is help out there. Your college campus will have healthcare clinics and trained staff to help you get through these times. Plus, calling home to whine to Mom is, of course, still allowed.

Medical Supplies

Having a few supplies stocked in your "medicine cabinet" will help you deal with minor illnesses. Buy a little Tupperware- or Rubbermaid-type container to store your medical supplies. Stocking this container with bandages, cough drops, decongestants, and headache and fever reducers are all good to start with. If you are commonly afflicted with certain illnesses (for example, colds or sore throats), be prepared for those illnesses striking in college. Keep the medications you have learned work best for you. Buy a thermometer so that you can take your own temperature when you are feeling feverish. Knowing if you have a fever will help you decide if and when you need professional medical attention. If you call the school clinic and talk to a nurse about your symptoms, it is always helpful if you can tell him or her what your temperature is.

Having a can of chicken soup stocked away for times your stomach is upset or you feel the flu coming on is always a good idea. If you have other similar comfort foods (such as pretzels, noodles, or 7-Up™) that you can easily keep on hand, stock those items as well. If you are sick, you will not feel like running to the store for a bottle of Sprite or Gatorade or to get a box of Jell-O.

Getting Medical Attention

If you get sick and your medicine cabinet is not doing the trick or if you are sick for more than two days, you need to seek medical attention. Know what your medical insurance policy is, and be familiar with whom to call in case you are sick, before you are faced with an illness. If you have campus insurance, you will be seen by the campus medical staff. If you are on your parents' insurance policy, find out who you can see local to your campus when you get sick. If you do not already, be sure to get annual physicals to ward off more serious or long-term conditions, such as high blood pressure or cholesterol.

Do not rely on premed students or nursing majors to diagnose your illness. They are in school just as you are. They may know more about illnesses than you do, but they are not trained professionals. Seek real help when you are sick. Do not rely on WebMD® or other online resources to self-diagnose your illness either. You might find useful information online, but you should not be relying on those sources for treatment or diagnosis.

If you get medical attention, listen to the treatment you are given. If you are given antibiotics, be sure to stick to the regime. Do not skip pills and stop taking your medication as soon as you start feeling better. Take all your medication even if you do not feel as if you need it anymore. You will start feeling better before the illness is completely gone; you will need to finish the medication to knock out the infection entirely. If you do not take all the medication prescribed, you run the risk of getting the same illness again and even developing a strand that is resistant to the antibiotic.

If you are attending college in an area of the country different than where you are accustomed, you may end up suffering from allergies that you never had before. There are more allergy medications available over the counter than ever before, but you will still need to consult medical professionals to determine which medication is best for you. Some medications may cause side effects such as drowsiness, so it might take a few tries of medicines to find the best one. Your doctor might give you samples at first to determine which medication you should take. Instead of spending money trying different over-the-counter meds, ask a doctor to recommend something for your specific symptoms and allergies.

Involvement

Your goal in college should be to graduate, of course, but also to get the most out of your college experience. To do this, you need to take advantage of all that your college has to offer. Do not sit around in your dorm room day after day or spend all your spare time talking to your friends and family back home. It is important to maintain ties with your home life and with your old friends, but you also need to get out there and meet new friends and experience new adventures. College is about learning. You should learn about your major area of study, yourself, and the world around you. Staring at the four walls of your dorm room is not what you need to be doing, and it certainly will not help you feel comfortable in your new environment or help you learn about yourself or the world around you. So, get out there, get involved, and have fun.

CHAPTER 15

Getting Involved

During your orientation, you likely received informational packets about different student organizations, clubs, and other extracurricular activities. These groups will help you meet new people and may even help you land your first job. Being involved in college life outside the classroom will help strengthen your résumé and may be the distinguishing factor that sets you apart from other qualified job applicants.

Student Government

You might have been involved in your high school's student body organization. If so, you may know for sure you want to be involved in the student government in your college. If you did not get involved in your high school's study body government, do not rule this out just yet. Your college's student government will be different than it was in high school. Whereas high school student presidents were most likely selected solely on popularity, there is no popular group in your first year in college — at least not yet. You are back on a level playing field, and if you are attending a large school, popularity will have nothing to do with the competition. If you are interested in government, politics, or even business and becoming a leader, the student government may be an excellent goal for you.

Most colleges will have the top positions in the student government filled by returning students but more often than not reserve spots for first-year students. If there are not specific slots open for freshmen or if all the seats are filled, check into running for a senate slot. You will be forced to meet people by running for a position in the student government. Most processes begin with a required number of signatures on a petition to allow you to enter the race. Most students will gladly sign a petition for you, even if they just met you. Do not feel like you can ask only people you knew before you decided to run. Get out there and meet your classmates. Tell them why you want to run, and ask for their support.

After you get your petition signed and are an official candidate in the race, you will need to start campaigning. Most schools will not have a budget for student races, so any fliers, posters, or signs you create will come out of your own pocket. Be creative in your campaigning. Use school message boards to post a bio of yourself, and tell your classmates what you hope to accomplish if you are elected to a position. If there are online message boards for your school, take advantage of the free advertising. Ask your friends, roommates, and suitemates to help you make posters, create slogans, and distribute fliers around campus.

Take note that getting elected is only the first step. If you are elected to a position, you will have responsibilities with your title. Make sure you have the time to commit to this activity before you jump into it. There will be mandatory meetings and projects that you will have to complete on your own time. Although rewarding, you might find the time commitment of your college's student body cuts into your study or free time too much. If you like the idea of being a part of the student body but you are scared off by the time commitment, see if your dorm has a group that you can get involved with. Some residence halls have councils that meet to discuss dorm issues and even vote on important dormitory concerns. The council might also help plan social events for your dorm.

Specialty Clubs and Organizations

Colleges have academic-focused clubs and also niche and specific interest clubs. There might be a chess, spelunking, and/or bowling club. The number of clubs available to you will depend mostly on the size of your school and how active the other students in your school are with the clubs. Finding a club that interests you should not be an issue. Finding only one club that interests you might be the problem. Scan message boards around campus and look at fliers posted around to try and find a group that sparks your interest.

Many college campuses have academic clubs. These clubs can be based on highest GPAs in the school or fields of study. Many major fields of study have clubs specifically designed for students with that major to meet and discuss concerns about that specific field. Foreign languages frequently have their own clubs as well. If you were in French or Spanish club in high school and plan on continuing in that foreign language, you should look into joining that club in college. Getting together with other people and speaking the language you are learning is an excellent way to practice for class and can be loads of fun. Most times, these clubs host events to showcase the language and culture the members are studying. Even if you are not in the club, if you get invited to a social gathering of a foreign language club, you should go. They are by and large educational, fun, and can offer some good food.

Other groups are separated out by interests or hobbies. You may not have to be an art major to join an art appreciation club. If you enjoy biking, hiking, or running, see if there is club for your specific interest, hobby, or passion. Your campus may also have organizations for gay, lesbian, bisexual, and transgender students and also students who wish to support them. Most campuses are filled with these special-interest clubs. Ask around, check message boards, and try to find a group that best fits your interests. When you meet people on campus who share a similar interest with you, ask them if they know of any clubs around campus that are based around that common interest.

If you cannot find a group for the area of your interest or passion, start your own. If you can find enough other students interested in joining the group you want to start, you can petition your school for funding for your group. Starting your own organization will give you solid leadership skills and will look amazing on your résumé. Find out your school's policy about starting new clubs, and go for it. Start polling your friends, classmates, and the people at the cafeteria table next to you to find out if there is anyone else interested in your hobby or passion. Start gathering names, even before you know if you will have enough people interested in joining the group. Get the contact information of people who do express an interest so that if you do get the club approved and started, you will be able to contact those people again for possible board members or at least participants in the group. If it does not work out, you truly have not lost anything, and you can feel proud of yourself that you tried to create a new group.

Service-Oriented Groups

Community service is always a good way to enhance your résumé while making you feel good about yourself and your contribution to society. You may have already joined a volunteer group or community service organization while you were in high school. If you are not currently affiliated with a community service organization or have not been in the past and would like to be, there are always service groups available at college campuses to join.

Examples of groups oriented toward service include:

- **Big Brothers, Big Sisters** focuses on mentoring youth through one-on-one interaction (**www.bbbs.org**).

- **Circle K:** Sponsored by a Kiwanis club, Circle K, according to its Web site, "is a co-educational service, leadership development, and friendship organization" (**www.circlek.org**).

- **Habitat for Humanity:** This nonprofit organization is a Christian housing ministry that helps provide safe housing to those in need (**www.habitat.org**).

- **Alpha Phi Omega:** A fraternity with more than 17,000 male and female members, this organization's goal is to develop leadership and promote friendship (**www.apo.org**).

If community service interests you and your campus does not offer a group that appeals to you, get involved with the local chapter of a charity organization that speaks to your heart. Some examples of other organizations or types of organizations that might interest you include:

- Homeless shelters

- Animal shelters or no-kill animal rescue and adoption agencies

- Public libraries

- Literacy programs

- Domestic violence shelters

- Food banks

Charities exist for just about every cause out there. Search the Internet for a program that interests you most and find out what volunteer opportunities it has available. You might be able to work remotely to help a cause or volunteer for fund-raising activities when your schedule allows. If the organization you wish to contribute to does not have a local chapter on your campus or in the community around your campus, you might consider volunteering to help start one. The initiative will be appreciated by the organization and will also look exceptional on your résumé.

Religious Organizations

If you have strong religious views or come from a strong religious background, you may want to find students with similar beliefs and backgrounds to share your experiences. If you are not religious but want to learn more about a certain religion or certain religious beliefs, you can search out clubs that share the same interest as you. You might find opportunities to join a board of a religious organization if it is something you are passionate about.

These groups arrange discussions and events based on their religious beliefs and holidays. The organizations might also aim to teach others about their religion and beliefs. Whatever your religious background of beliefs, you might find a club that supports your same beliefs and religious system. Having a group of friends with beliefs similar to you is a solid support system for when you are going through rough times or struggle with defending your beliefs to others who may not understand them.

Cultural Organizations

If you are a foreign student or even if you just have a cultural background that you are proud of or want to learn more about, you might want to join an organization made up of students who share your culture. Joining a cultural organization should help you learn more about your own culture and also other cultures around you. Use the knowledge you gain to educate others on your culture and be more understanding of cultures different from your own. Message boards around campus are good places to look for these groups.

Student Activities Office

Depending on the size of your campus, you might find different student activities occurring every day of the week. Attending these events can be fun and an excellent way to meet other people. If you are a social creature and love to plan events, you might even want to join the planning committees for some of the events sponsored by the student activities office. If you have ideas for ways to get students together, to have fun, and to meet others, this organization might be the perfect match for you.

This office will have staff advisors who help students form committees and plan events. You will assist in managing the budget for the event you are planning. Because these events are sponsored by the student activities office (that student activity fee you pay each semester), there is normally a fairly decent-sized budget. The experience of planning some of the school's largest events will be fun and give you valuable experience managing a large project. This organization will also give you major points on your résumé, especially if you are going into a field where financial management skills are important.

You might be helping plan the fall and spring festivals, the formal dances, concerts, and other fun events that take place throughout the year. If you are interested in this opportunity, contact the student activities office and ask what committees have openings. When you are first getting involved in the group, you might want to stick to the smaller events and committees. If you want to have more of a say in how an event is planned, start by joining a small committee. You will get more experience in the entire process of planning and managing a budget, and you also may find that your suggestions are more likely to get heard and to be implemented than if you try to jump into a large event with a huge committee.

Attendee

If you are not ready to join a committee or an organization in your first year, start by attending events put on by the various organizations around campus. If you find a group that you enjoy more than the others or that you find you are always attending its events, you might end up volunteering with it or joining the organization. If not, being an active participant is still a good way to get involved in the campus and community around you.

If you find you are interested in many different organizations, try a few of them out before you decide to join one, or support many different organizations by actively participating in their events and recruiting other friends to join you in their events. As long as you are not holed up in your dorm room and you are out around campus enjoying yourself and meeting other people, you will be getting a much richer college experience — the type of experience you should have during your freshman year of school. Find your spot, the group where you fit in the best, but also explore groups that you want to learn more about. Broaden your horizons and learn more about yourself and those around you.

Case Study: Getting Involved on Your Campus

Alan Acosta, Residence Coordinator
University Housing, Florida State University

Alan Acosta said there are many ways for freshmen to meet other students and get involved. If a student lives on campus, the residence hall will have many opportunities to get involved, whether that is by meeting floormates, hanging out with the RA, going to social events, or participating in the residence hall association.

But no matter where a student lives, the institution's campus activities office will have many student organizations available. Many students choose to get involved in social Greek organizations, but there are also student organizations based on academic interests. Acosta advised that if freshmen make the effort, they should be able to find ways to get connected to the campus.

Eric Booth, M.A., Director of Residence Life
Reinhardt College

Eric Booth said students should take the time to join or start a campus organization to meet people. He advised that shy students work with their RA to help plug in to the residence hall programs.

Kelly R. Doel, Area Coordinator
University of Central Florida

Most colleges and universities take pride in offering a variety of involvement opportunities for students, including student government, intramural sports, academic honor societies, sororities/fraternities, and interest-based clubs, according to Kelly Doel. Commonly, colleges have an office that focuses solely on student involvement, and its Web site provides contact information for every club on campus. She said students can choose their level of involvement by attending meetings or taking on leadership roles within organizations. Living on campus, she said, provides unique opportunities such as getting involved with area councils or learning more about the RA position. Her tip to freshmen is to take

Case Study: Getting Involved on Your Campus

advantage of these opportunities, as some may lead to interests that result in a career path.

Ashley Chittum, Sophomore
Tennessee Wesleyan College

Ashley Chittum said even small campuses will offer many events for students to get involved in. She said that students should check the tents on tables in the cafeteria, as many schools post the week's upcoming events there.

Carolynn S. Nath, Area Coordinator
University of Central Florida

Carolynn Nath said students should get involved early and to also go to activity and organization fairs that occur at orientation and during the first few weeks of school. She said students should go to different meetings for different organizations and see what fits them best. Students need to experience new cultures, ways of thought, and activities. She cautions students to not get over involved as a freshman to maintain a healthy work/school/social balance.

Students who cannot find a club or organization that fits them should start their own. They can do so for free and will have the opportunity to make their own bylaws for the club/organization and manage its account.

Matthew Gramling, Sophomore
Oglethorpe College

Matthew Gramling's college has a mandatory program for freshmen to help them get involved on and off campus. He said he has visited local museums, helped clean up a local cemetery, and participated in food drives through this program. He also said students get to know other students on these events. Although he may not come away from an event with a new friend, he will get to know more students that he might bump into on campus and develop a friendship with later.

Frederica Anderson, Sophomore
Savannah College of Art and Design

Frederica Anderson said college life is not all books and work. Her proof is the

Case Study: Getting Involved on Your Campus

amount of social activities that colleges offer throughout the year. She said events such as movie nights, ice cream socials, costume parties, and prom nights offer students fun ways to get involved on campus. To find out about these events, she said students should simply check around campus for posters advertising the events.

James Johns, Professional Student
Georgia Highlands College

Although a social person, James Johns said he is loner at heart. He participated in activities but was not there to make friends. He suggested students talk to their counselor to find some fun programs.

CHAPTER 16

It is All Greek to You

The most well-known social organizations on campus are the fraternities and sororities. If you are considering joining a Greek organization, be sure to do your research to make sure it is the right decision. If you have older siblings, friends, or family members that were in Greek organizations, ask them what they liked and disliked about being in the organization. Find out what they think would be best for you, and ask them if they did it over again, would they still join a fraternity or sorority? Be realistic about what you can expect to give and get from joining a Greek organization. Ignore all the movies that stereotype such organizations. Find out the facts and make a well-educated decision about whether you should join. If you never thought about joining a Greek organization, please do not skip this chapter. Even if you maintain your position about not joining, you may learn a few things about what these organizations are all about.

Pros of the Greek Life

Wild parties and no schoolwork are the two biggest advantages of joining a Greek organization. All right, I am joking. But watch a few movies and television shows and you would think it is true; that is the biggest and most misleading stereotype of Greek organizations. Greek organizations encourage leadership, community involvement, and campus leadership roles. You will often find that Greek members hold the highest offices in the student government and other elite positions on campus — and it is not because they throw the best parties.

Joining a fraternity or sorority means you are automatically in a new family. You have brothers and sisters in your organization that you will bond extremely closely to and may remain lifelong friends with, long after college is over. You will also continue to meet new brothers and sisters as you go out beyond your college years. As a freshman entering college, you can often feel alone and like you have no friends or family around you. Joining a fraternity or sorority is like creating an instant family around you: you are not alone anymore. Depending on your school and chapter, you might be living in the same house with your fraternity or sorority members. You will get to know them all that much better and quicker in these settings and also will have older members more readily available for mentoring.

Being in the same Greek family with someone, even a complete stranger, creates an immediate bond. You will have a common background. Your network of allies just increased. If you enjoy camaraderie with others and want the close bond of a family away from home, Greek organizations might be something to consider. When you graduate college and start your job search, you will find this resource valuable.

Fraternities and sororities breed leaders and encourage members to become leaders with their own organization and also the campus and community. As a member of a Greek organization, you will have the opportunity to mentor younger students and take up leadership roles as you progress through your college years. Many organizations hold workshops to help cultivate these leadership skills in their members and teach these members effective management and leadership skills.

Community service tops the list of what Greek organizations are all about. Chapters might support one specific cause that they dedicate their time and service to supporting. Participating in such community-service events is a good résumé boost and can be attractive to employers after graduation. You can also get a sense of satisfaction in helping the community and world around you. If you find a Greek chapter that is supporting an organization you believe deeply in, you will find the friendship and the charity work both to be rewarding.

Scholastically, Greek organizations provide an excellent support system to their members and take scholastics seriously, contrary to what is often depicted in movies. If you are a member of a Greek organization, you will have excellent support academically. Depending on the chapter you join, you might have access to a library full of notes from lectures and test study guides that are organized by a professor or course. You might even have an older student in the organization tutor you in a class or subject that you are struggling to make the grade in. Study groups are often available in your chapter.

Cons of the Greek Life

Of course, there are disadvantages to joining a fraternity or sorority. One of the biggest reasons you may not want to join a Greek organization is the large time commitment that the groups require of their members. You have to be committed to the organization, and that means you are required to attend meetings, seminars, and formal events held by the chapter. Your Greek organization will become a huge part of your life. If you were planning on participating in other campus activities or sports, you may not have the time necessary to commit to the group. Before you decide to get involved with a Greek organization, be sure you understand the time commitment it demands and see how that fits in to your plan for college and your time schedule for other activities.

Another huge disadvantage for most people considering joining a fraternity or sorority is the rush or hazing that takes places as initiation in the organization. Most campuses have policies against Greek organizations hazing new members, but more often than not, the organizations still have some form of embarrassing activities that new members must go through while pledging. If you are interested in joining a certain chapter of Greek organization on your campus, ask around about its hazing rituals. If you find out it requires new members to take part in dangerous rituals or activities that you do not agree with, find another chapter that does not take part in such things. Although you may be expected to do certain things to prove you want to join and to show that you understand the oath of the chapter, you should not be asked to do anything you are uncomfortable with or that goes against the chapter's own motto.

Fraternities and sororities are not free. If you want to join, ask about the dues you will be expected to pay to be a member of the organization. Besides the dues, you may end up paying for other activities such as parties throughout the year. There will be times you will have to buy gifts for certain members of the group and other random items that come up throughout the year. Be aware and ask questions before you join about how much will be expected of you in dues and incidentals to be sure you can fit the fraternity or sorority into your budget. Also, ask if scholarships are available through the chapter to help cover the dues.

If you are still interested in joining a fraternity or sorority, take a close look at your own personality. If you like to keep to yourself and are not that social, you might want to reconsider joining a Greek organization. If you are not comfortable being around large groups and prefer having only a few close friends, you may not be best suited for the Greek life. If, on the other hand, you thrive in social settings and love surrounding yourself with huge groups of people that all know you, you may have found your new home. If missing social events would crush you and you are looking to find a network of friends that will stick by your side for life, then a fraternity or sorority might just be the answer you have been looking for since you decided to go to college.

Making the Decision

Weigh the pros and cons of joining a Greek organization carefully before you make your final decision. Ask questions about the various chapters at your school. Research the history of the chapter you are most interested in joining. Look up information about the specific Greek organization online and ask questions around campus about the chapter before you make a final decision to pledge.

Ask for advice from anyone you know who has been or is currently in a fraternity or sorority, and if the person knows you well, ask if he or she thinks you would be right for that life style. Revisit your mission statement for your college experience. Honestly evaluate whether you think a Greek organization would fit into your vision. If it does not, ask yourself what you are willing, if anything, to give up to make that life fit in to your mission statement or, if after carefully weighing this option, you are willing to change you mission statement to include Greek life into it.

Do not go out and watch *Animal House* or some other stereotypical Greek party-hardy depiction. When you are making your decision about whether this life style is right for you, be sure you are basing your decision on factual data and not the stereotypes.

For more information regarding fraternities and sororities check out: **http://en.wikipedia.org/wiki/Fraternities_and_sororities** or **www. greekpages.com**.

Case Study: Sorority Advice

Ashley Chittum, Member of the Sigma Kappa Sorority

Although Ashley Chittum considered joining a sorority before she started college, she did not make the decision to join until the second semester of her freshman year. She said her sorority has rules against drinking and participates in volunteer work, including a memory walk.

Students considering joining a Greek organization should know that being a member of a sorority or fraternity takes up much time, according to Chittum. She said her organization has meetings twice a week. Before joining an organization, Chittum said students should find out as much as possible about the chapter they are considering joining. They should know the history of the organization, what that organization stands for and is based on, whether it is a national or local chapter, and the rules about initiation. Chittum's sorority has anti-hazing rules.

Finances

Money will be tight in college, well, for most freshmen anyway. You may have student loans. Your parents might have even taken out loans for you to go to school. You may be living on bare minimum or even on credit at times because all your money is going into paying tuition and book fees. Some of you may have to work part-time or full-time to finance your education and be able to eat at the same time. Without planning ahead, you can land yourself in a financial world of trouble. The next two chapters will discuss common financial pitfalls and how to avoid them. They will also give budgeting tips and include information on how to juggle work and school and try to have a semi-decent social life at the same time.

CHAPTER 17

Watch your Assets: Budgeting and Finances

By now in your life, you may have a savings account at least and, better yet, a checking account too. If not, do not worry. This chapter will give you information on how to start one and tell you why you need one. If you think that because your parents are paying for your college education that you can skip this chapter, think again. You will need money for incidentals, which are fun things like movies, eating out, and concerts; personal hygiene products; groceries for your dorm room; and school supplies.

Checking and Savings Accounts

Let us assume that you do not have a checking or savings account. Maybe you have never even stepped foot in a bank before in your life; you need to get in there. If you decide to get a credit card — which comes up later in this chapter — you will need a checking account to pay your bill every month. You will also need a place to store your petty cash so that you are not walking around with all your money all the time. You cannot store your cash under your mattress either, as it might just wind up missing one day. A bank offers security for your money, and if you have large amounts of money, you can earn interest on it by keeping it in a bank.

Checking accounts rarely earn any interest, or they earn little interest. Savings accounts, on the other hand, earn a higher interest rate, though most savings accounts still only earn a small amount of interest. Before signing up for a checking or savings account, ask the bank what the interest rate is for these accounts. Most people will have both a savings and checking account. The savings account should be used to save money for big purchases or long-term goals. The checking account is useful for buying smaller items and paying bills on a monthly basis. You can open savings and checking accounts with the same bank or different banks. If you have both accounts with the same bank, it will be easier to transfer money back and forth, if that is something you will need to do often. Depending on which bank you do business with, you may be able to transfer money from your checking account to your savings account or vice versa, even if the two accounts are at different banks. You should check with your bank on this and be aware that the transfer may not be immediate.

When you open an account, whether checking or savings, be sure to read the fine print. Ask about additional charges and fees. Some banks limit the number of transactions you can make per month. Some banks may have a minimum-balance requirement and will charge you monthly fees if your balance drops below the minimum. Find out up front about the fees a bank might charge. Ask about different account options. Most banks offer a few different types of checking accounts. If you are not carrying a large balance, ask about a "free" checking account. By and large, these accounts will not limit the number of transactions you can have per month. Some accounts have an overdraft protection feature that can be added. With overdraft protection, banks typically give customers a specific number of times in which they will not be charged overdraft fees for overdrawing their checking accounts. After this, customers will be charged the overdraft fee each time their accounts are in the negative.

Check Cards/Debit Cards

Depending on your bank, you might have the option to have a check or debit card, which are basically the same thing. This card can be used at an automated teller machine (ATM) but also carries a credit card logo, normally a Visa or MasterCard symbol. These cards can be swiped as a debit card, where you enter your ATM pin number in the system, or they can be used like a credit card without entering your pin number. Bear in mind that no matter which option you choose when using this card, the money will be drafted from your checking account. If you do not have the money in your account to pay for the purchase, do not buy it. You will overdraft your account and get charged large fees for charging more than you have in available funds.

A warning about check cards: According to consumer advocate Clark Howard, check cards are fake credit cards. He said that these cards masquerade as real credit cards but offer none of the protection that a real credit card does. A real credit card offers a 90-day dispute period on charges; a check card does not. If you use your check card for certain purchases such as gas and hotels, you may have a hold put on your account for much more than the purchase amount. For more information on check cards, visit **http://en.wikipedia.org/wiki/Debit_card** or **http://clarkhoward.com/shownotes/category/7/40/225/**.

Small, Large, and Online Banks

There are different options when it comes to banks. Banks come in all different shapes and sizes. You can choose from mega-banks, small community banks, credit unions, and online banks. Each of these options will offer advantages and disadvantages. It is important for you to weigh the options of each type of bank and find the one that is right for you. Shop around at different banks and find one that feels most comfortable. You might find one bank where you truly like the branch manager, even though you did not think you would like the type of bank he works in.

Small Banks

Your hometown or college town might have a local community bank or a bank with a few branches in just the local area. Small banks often offer more personal service and attention. If you make a mistake on your accounting and accidentally overdraw your account, a small bank is more likely to forgive the mistake and reverse the charge. The disadvantage of small banks is that they might not have all the service options of a larger bank. A small bank might not have the online banking option that a larger bank would offer.

Make an appointment with the branch manager before you decide to bank with it. If the bank is extremely small, you might be talking to the branch manager without even realizing it. Ask about the bank's policies on different issues that arise — such as if you accidentally overdraft your account. Gauge the branch manager's personality. If he or she is not that helpful before you open an account, chances are the bank will not be helpful when you are a customer either. Pick a bank where you feel most comfortable with its employees and branch manager.

Large Banks

Some refer to these banks as mega-banks. These banks might have branches covering a large region or even the nation. You will most likely have numerous options for accounts and loans. You will also have the benefit of more ATM and bank locations. If you travel, having a large bank might come in handy. Banking out of town will be easier, and you may not have to travel out of your way to find an approved ATM. Most of these banks will have a comprehensive online banking option. Unlike a smaller bank, mega-banks may not offer personal attention. You might have a harder time meeting with the branch manager or might run into more red tape when trying to get an issue resolved.

If you choose a large bank, meet with the branch manager first. See how easy it is to meet with the manager before an issue arises, and ask about how the bank handles issues. Ask around your area and find out what other people think about that bank. Chances are you will meet plenty of people in your area who use the same bank — that does not mean the bank is a good one. Ask them if they like the bank. Ask them if they ever had an issue and how that bank resolved it. The bureaucracy of a large bank can sometimes be overwhelming and can lead to frustration later on.

Online Banks

Some banks are entirely online. These banks have no "brick and mortar" buildings. That means there is no office for you to visit and do your banking; all the services are available online. Two of the most popular online banks are ING and Immigrant Savings and Loan. These banks are insured, just the same as traditional banks, and offer the same selection of services as most traditional banks offer. The advantage of these banks is that they often offer higher interest rates for savings and checking accounts and often have fewer fees associated with them. They do have toll-free numbers that customers can call for person-to-person attention, but they do not have any office or branch that customers can visit.

If you accomplish most of your banking online already or are planning on doing most of your banking online, these banks might be a good choice for you. You will be able to pay bills, transfer money, and set up automatic bill pay through these banks. Check on the bank's ATM use policy before you make a decision. Many online banks offer free ATM services through a certain teller company. You should be able to search approved ATM locations online to see the availability of ATMs in your area.

Account at Home

If you already have an account with your hometown bank, whether it is a checking account, savings account, or both, there is no real need to open a new account with a bank close to your college. To start, check to see if your local bank has a branch near your college. If not, make sure you are signed up for online banking; however, realize that if you have checks to deposit and the account is not in town this may become a problem. Most banks offer almost a complete line of services online and free of charge. Find out about this option and make sure you are enrolled, if available, before you leave for college.

Also, ask your bank or check online to see if there are any local ATMs in your college town. Ask about ATM surcharges if you use another bank's machine. ATM charges can add up quickly. Most banks charge between $2 and $4, and you may be charged by both banks — which could equal up to $8 for one transaction. Before you start using other bank ATMs, find out about the fees. You might find your bank account whittled away by finance charges

Credit Cards

College students are flooded with credit card offers. Some students even start getting offers in the mail before graduating high school. After you turn 18 years old, many credit companies will start soliciting you to open a credit card account. There are plenty of good reasons why you should get a credit card, but with credit cards comes a large responsibility. You can end up causing much more trouble for yourself while you are in college and for years after you graduate if you are not careful about opening credit cards and using them.

Credit cards allow you to purchase items now and pay for them later. Most cards come with a certain grace period, where, if you pay off the balance in full with each bill, you will not be charged any interest on the purchases. If you do not pay your balance in full each month, you will be paying interest on your total balance. In essence, you will be paying more than sticker price for the items you purchased earlier. If someone told you that he or she would let you buy a gallon of milk, marked at $2.50, for $3, you would laugh. But that is what credit card companies do, and people blindly go along with it.

As a college student, credit cards should be used for only two reasons: emergency situations and to build credit. Emergency situations constitute your car being broken down on the side of the road and needing a tow truck or your late-night visit to the emergency room. Not having the cash to pay for a concert that you truly want to see is not an emergency. If you use your credit card too freely, you might find yourself in more debt than your college loans — and you will have enough of those. Building credit is an important reason to have a credit card. If you use your card for small purchases, keep track of what you spend, and pay it off at the end of the month, you will start building a good credit history. Your credit will be checked at numerous times in your life, such as renting your first apartment after graduation. Having a good credit rating and history will help you in the long run when making big purchases too, such as a house or car.

Shop around for credit cards. Read the terms and conditions to find out what interest rate the card is charging you, just in case you ever have to run a balance on the card. Check to see if there is an annual fee just to hold the card. You should be able to find a card with a reasonable interest rate and no annual fee. Many cards also offer rewards programs. Some of these programs offer airline miles, cash back, or other discounts and benefits. Be sure to read through the terms of rewards cards. Commonly, the rewards are not as good as the initial offer makes them out to be. Do not feel limited by just the offers you receive in the mail. Check online for other offers — **www.bankrate.com** compares offers from many different credit card companies.

Credit cards can be a dangerous thing in college, and if you do not use them carefully, you could be paying interest on purchases made during college long after graduation. Racking up credit card debt and only making minimum payments can lead to future credit issues. It is important to make sure that you can pay off the purchases that you charge to your credit card each month. If you cannot pay off the purchases when your monthly bill is due, it is best not to pay for items using a credit card. In case of a large emergency purchase that cannot be paid off by your next bill, it is important to come up with a budget for paying off that charge within a reasonable amount of time. If you only make minimal payments each month, it may take you years to pay off a large purchase because you will only be paying on the monthly interest and never on the principal. Having a credit card is not a bad choice if you are trying to build good credit, but having a maxed-out credit card will hurt your credit score and cause many issues down the road, such as not being able to buy a car or house.

Budgeting

If you are not an accounting major or if numbers make you nervous, do not freak out. Budgeting does not require an in-depth knowledge of economics. It is quite simple: Spend less than you bring in. If you spend more than you bring in, your budget will bust. If you are not making any money, your budget might be to spend less than your parents give you. Creating a simple budget should be doable for most college students.

To begin a budget, make a list of areas that you will be spending money on. These areas might include: car expenses (gas, insurance, maintenance), entertainment, eating out, school supplies, laundry, toiletries, snacks, and clothes. Next, list your monthly income, whether from a part-time job or an allowance from your parents. Go through your list of expenses, and estimate how much money you will spend on each area. Add up your total estimated expenses, then subtract the total expenses from your total income. If you have a negative number, your budget needs to be adjusted. Go back through your expenses and start cutting until you reach a positive number. If you leave a cushion, you will have room for unexpected expenses. When creating your expense list, be sure to include a savings or rainy day fund. You never know when you will have an unexpected car repair or want to spend extra one month on entertainment when your favorite band comes to town.

Go through the budget worksheet in Appendix A. Your original budget might need to be amended after you implement it. You might find you spend less on gas and more on food than you originally planned. If you are having trouble guessing how much you will spend each month on expenses, take one month to keep track of all your purchases. Get a small notebook that you can carry around with you. Each time you spend money, whether getting a soda from a machine or buying gas for your car, write it down. At the end of the month, add up how much you spent on each area and use that as a guide for your budget. If your parents are good at budgeting (and not all parents are), ask them to help you create your budget. Your school might offer a class on budgeting as well. Check into what your college offers in the way of help for you to keep on top of your finances.

Your Credit Score

Paying your bills on time and being a responsible owner of a credit card will help you establish good credit history. Your credit history and credit score (a number used to show creditors how good you are at paying your bills on time and not overusing your credit line) will help you buy houses, cars, rent apartments, and even get hired in the future (yes, potential employers may check applicants' credit history before hiring them). Many different companies will check your credit during your life and will use your credit number to determine if you are eligible to buy from them and what interest rate they will charge you in a loan. Having a good credit number will make your purchases easier and will cost you less in interest.

You should be aware of your credit score and history so that you can negotiate loans, ensure no one has used your credit fraudulently, and to be able to dispute any erroneous matters on your report. There are three credit-reporting companies nationwide: Equifax, Experian, and TransUnion. Every 12 months, you are entitled to a free copy of your credit report from each of these three companies. Beware: Many companies, including banks and credit card companies, will try to sell you your credit report. You can get the same information for free if you are responsible enough to keep track of your own finances. Go to **www.annualcreditreport.com** to obtain your free credit report from each of the three reporting agencies. If you pull your credit report from one of the three credit agencies every four months, you can keep track of your credit throughout the year without paying a thing. For instance, in January, pull your Experian credit report, in April, pull your TransUnion report, and in August, pull your Equifax report.

Your actual credit score is a number between 300 and 850 that helps potential lenders rate your risk as a borrower. If you want to get your credit score with your free annual credit report, you will have to pay for it. Through Equifax, you can purchase your Fair Isaac Corporation (FICO) score for $7.95. If you are planning on buying a car or home, check your credit score and report about six months before you plan to make the purchase. If there are any discrepancies on your report, you will have time to correct them before you start applying for loans. A score higher than 700 is commonly considered good. To have no issues obtaining credit and getting the best interest rate possible, aim to have a score higher than 750. For more information on credit scores, what the number means, and how to improve your number, check out **www.myfico.com** or **www.clarkhoward.com**.

Paying for College

Financing your college education can be a tricky task. As a college freshman, you will be faced with many options on how you can pay for the next four (or more) years. Understanding these options fully can be daunting and time consuming. While this book will not fully explain all college loan and scholarship options, it will offer a basic understanding of loan options and refer you to resources to explore loan and scholarship options more fully.

The first step in finding the best loan option for you is to understand the three basic types of loans. College loans can be categorized as Federal or private loans, and Federal loans can be broken down further into Federal Student loans and Federal Parent loans. Within these main categories are many different loan options. Some loans require immediate repayment while others defer payment until after graduation or until the time that you leave school if you do not graduate. Likewise, some loans start accumulating interest immediately while others defer interest charges until graduation or until the time that you leave school if you do not graduate. Be sure to research loan options and terms thoroughly before you decide on what loans are best for you.

Federal Student loans are guaranteed by the government and offer favorable terms to the borrower. In the name of the student (not your parents), these loans often carry low interest rates. To qualify, a student must first complete the Free Application for Federal Student Aid (FAFSA). Loans are awarded based on need (calculated through income of the student and parents). Credit scores are not taken into account when these loans are awarded. The two main types of Federal Student loans are Stafford and Perkins loans. A Stafford loan can be either subsidized or unsubsidized. Subsidized loans are more favorable since the U.S. Department of Education pays the interest on the loan while the student is in school and through any grace period allowed by the loan (usually six months after a student graduates or leaves school). To qualify, students must be enrolled in college at least part time. A Perkins loan is awarded to students considered by the government to have "exceptional" need. This low interest loan is similar to the subsidized Stafford loan with the added benefits of having no fees and a longer grace period for repayment.

Federal Parent loans, also guaranteed by the Federal government, are in the name of the student's parent. The Federal Parent PLUS loan is not awarded based on need. A credit check of the parents will determine eligibility and the loan is set with a fixed interest rate. A FAFSA must be completed to determine eligibility for these loans and the money usually is sent directly to the school, not the student or the parents. Interest paid on these loans may be tax deductible for the parents. Terms of parental loans are usually not as favorable as the student loans. The interest rates are slightly higher and there is no deferment of repayment or of interest while the student is enrolled in school. Ultimately, the parent, not the student, is responsible for repayment of these loans.

Private student loans are any loans not guaranteed by the Federal government. These loans vary widely in interest rates and repayment stipulations. A student's credit score is often used to determine eligibility and the interest rate charged on these loans. Offered through your college or through private financial institutions, these loans can be used to make up the difference in what Federal loans you are awarded and the cost of your education. Check the loan terms carefully before signing a promissory note for private loans. Federal loans will usually offer more favorable terms and should be taken first, with private loans looked at as a last option.

The first step for all students needing financial aid is to complete the FAFSA (**www.fafsa.ed.gov**) before the school year starts (usually due by the June before your school year begins). This form must be resubmitted each year you attend school. Freshmen should also visit their college's financial aid office for more information on loans and grants or scholarships. Grants and scholarships are the best way to finance your college career since they do not have to be repaid. Be sure to start your search for grants and scholarships early as some require essays or other information and could have early deadlines. Other great resources for student financial aid and scholarships information include: **www.salliemae.com** (offers Federal and private loans for students and parents as well as helpful information on the different types of loans available); **www.finaid.org** (offers loan calculators, a Student Loan Checklist, and tons of information on the types of loans available); **www.safeborrowing.com** (offers information on student loans, credit cards, mortgages, and other types of debt to help consumers use credit wisely); **www.fastweb.com** (offers a free search of scholarships and other financial aid for college); and **www. collegeboard.org** (offers information on financial aid options and a scholarship search).

Planning for Your Future

Even though you have just begun your college career and money will be tight, it is not too early to start planning ahead for future purchases and even for your retirement. One of the best ways to ensure you will have enough money to retire when you want to is to start saving early. Putting away just a little money over a long period of time is the best way to save for your future. Time is on your side when it comes to saving and growing your money wisely. If you start saving money now, you will have more of it later and will create good financial habits that will help you in the long run.

If at all possible, start a Roth IRA (individual retirement account). This retirement account allows you to save up to $5,000 per year if you are under 50 years old ($6,000 a year for those 50 years old or older). This money should be used to save for your retirement and should not be used as a savings account. There are fees and penalties for early withdrawal, so be sure the money you put in this account is money you do not plan on using until you are 59 and a half years old. As long as you are not making more than $100,000 a year, you are eligible for this retirement account. A Roth IRA allows you grow your money in an account where all interest earned is tax free and no taxes are charged when you withdraw it, as long as you do not make an early withdrawal.

Other retirement accounts are available, but most college students will find a Roth IRA the most advantageous to their situation. Clark Howard compares the different retirement accounts and their advantages on his Web site: **clarkhoward.com/topics/investing_guide.html**. Also on his Web site, Howard references a chart that shows just how much you can benefit from saving early. According to the chart, a 15-year-old can save $2,000 for seven years and be a millionaire by age 65. Do not take my word for it — check out the chart yourself at **http://clarkhoward.**

com/shownotes/category/7/13/220/379. For additional information on saving for your retirement, check out: **www.smartmoney.com/ retirement.**

If you do not have much money to start investing now, ask your family to help out. Your parents might be willing to match your investments to help encourage you to save for your future. You might also find that other family members (grandparents, aunts, and uncles) might be willing to contribute to your retirement account as birthday or holiday presents. These contributions will mean so much more than a sweater you will never wear, and they might feel better about giving you money for savings than sending you cash.

Case Study: Budgeting and Finances

Alan Acosta, Residence Coordinator
University Housing, Florida State University

Alan Acosta advised, "Be smart with your money." He recommended that students try to create a budget to manage their money wisely, and it should include all income and expenses.

Acosta also said that freshmen should start saving money now in a personal savings account and, if possible, a Roth IRA account, as this will be extremely helpful for the students' financial future.

Acosta warned that one big issue many freshmen struggle with is credit. He said freshmen should have a credit card only if they feel as if they can handle it responsibly. It can be extremely difficult to repair their credit if they abuse it early in their life. According to Acosta, students should never sign up for a credit card without understanding the responsibilities that come with it. There are campus services that can assist with financial issues. Also, students should visit their campus' career center. Acosta said that students not only can they learn what to do to get a good job after college, but they can also learn how to manage their money in an effective fashion.

Case Study: Budgeting and Finances

Eric Booth, M.A., Director of Residence Life
Reinhardt College

Eric Booth warned to beware of overspending on fast food, partying, and other social opportunities. He said that when creating a budget, students should realize that hidden or unexpected (such as car repairs) expenses may come up.

Kelly R. Doel, Area Coordinator
University of Central Florida

Kelly Doel said that budgeting can be quite challenging for college students, but it is beneficial for students to create a budget that is realistic and not too confining. It is a good idea to budget for the unexpected and take advantage of coupons and sales when possible. Even though it may be tough, starting to save money in college will prepare students for the mind-set of planning for the future instead of living in the now, she said. For students who are electronically minded, Doel suggested budgeting software such as Microsoft® Money and Quicken.

Ashley Chittum, Sophomore
Tennessee Wesleyan College

Ashley Chittum said that her parents give her a set amount of money each month, and she has to make sure that money will last her until the next month. She said students can stretch their budget by eating on campus and taking advantage of the free activities offered at their school, including ping-pong tables, sand volleyball competitions, pool tables, and campus-sponsored events.

Carolynn S. Nath, Area Coordinator
University of Central Florida

Carolynn Nath said that students will face challenges when it comes to financial accountability, which include having access to credit cards, managing bank accounts, receiving scholarship money or refund checks from financial aid, and not having enough money to pay for wants and needs. She said that by this time in their lives, students may not have managed multiple accounts or to this magnitude. Freshmen should know that it is extremely important for them to understand finances, regardless of whether their parents or guardians are

Case Study: Budgeting and Finances

managing money for them, according to Nath. Students need to learn as freshmen how to manage their finances, Nath advised, not when they graduate college, which she said often occurs. For freshmen that need spending money, Nath said students can earn extra money by working on campus. Jobs on campus are quite flexible and can pertain to their majors or be a side interest, including the fitness center on campus or tutoring. When it comes to budgeting, students must also realize the responsibility involved in having new financial freedoms, Nath said. Students need to bear in mind that scholarship monies or financial aid checks need to stretch out for the entire semester or year. She warned that students can see a huge lump sum of money and want to spend it on non-necessities and might end up having to take more loans or pinch pennies by mid-semester if they are not budgeting from the beginning.

Frederica Anderson, Sophomore
Savannah College of Art and Design

Frederica Anderson said that students need to save money, because school supplies are expensive. Students should look into classes and seminars offered on campus that focus on budgeting.

James Johns, Professional Student
Georgia Highlands College

Money is a problem for most students, James Johns said. Freshman should use their first year to learn how to balance their budget. His advice is for students not to spend all their money partying and end up with no money to buy food. He also said students should "Save, save, save!" Students should separate their wants from needs. Students need food, not need another Wii remote. If students need help with budgeting and finances, he suggested they take Economics 101 and Math 101, as those classes helped him.

Ryan Thompson, 2008 Graduate
Southern Polytechnic State University

College freshmen can maintain a good budget by keeping records on what they spend and staying focused on spending money on things they need rather than

Case Study: Budgeting and Finances

their wants, Ryan Thompson advised. Freshmen will have a tendency to ask their parents for financial assistance instead of developing their own independence. During his freshman year, Thompson needed his parents to financially assist him with school and additional expenses. He soon began to work part time. He made a goal to be financially independent of his parents by his sophomore year and created a path to reach that goal, including applying to be an RA to receive free room and board on campus. He also applied to work for the campus cafeteria, which meant he would be on a free meal plan. For more information on budgeting, Thompson said students should visit the career and counseling center.

CHAPTER 18

The Balancing Act: Work and College

Depending on your situation, you might be trying to hold down a job while you are a student. Some students will choose to work part time to have some extra spending money. Some will take on a part-time job because they need the extra money to pay for their living expenses. Other students might have to work full time to support themselves while they are in school. Whatever your situation, there are some things to know before you decide to take a job while you are a student. Plus, if you do not have any choice in the matter, this chapter might at least help you juggle your school, work, and social life without losing your mind.

If getting a job is something you are considering, be sure to weigh the pros and cons of working while a student. Your time will already be overtaxed with class, studying, and trying to maintain a social life. If you are trying to earn some extra cash to go out more, you might want to consider that having a job might give you the extra money, but it will be taking away the time you once had to go out. So, you might just find yourself in a catch-22 situation where if you do not work, you have the time but not the money to go out more, and if you do work, you will have the money but not the time. Try to at least make it through your first semester of school before you decide if you want to get a part-time job. After you have made it through one semester, you should have a more realistic idea of how much time you have, if any, to take on a job.

If you decide getting a part-time job is what you want to do or have to do to finance your college career, consider all your options for work. Some part-time jobs will be easier to juggle with school. Some jobs might help you decide on a major or career path. Some jobs will earn you more money with less time spent on the job. Weigh all your options carefully, and look into several possibilities before you commit to an employer. Try to avoid jumping from one job to another after only a few months. As a college student, you might change jobs frequently, but try to lessen job hopping as much as possible. Future employers might be wary of hiring you if you never keep a job more than a month or two.

Work-study Programs and On-Campus Jobs

Your college will likely offer work-study programs. These programs allow students to work on campus. Find out from your financial aid office if you are eligible for a work-study job, and find out what jobs are available. These jobs are frequently on campus. Some of these opportunities, such as working a desk or receptionist-type job, will allow you to study during work. Most programs limit the number of hours a week you can work so that you will not end up spending too many hours working to study.

Other jobs on campus might relate to your major. If you are majoring in journalism or communications, you might be able to work at your school's newspaper or radio station. These jobs will help you gain experience that will be helpful after school and give you some extra money while you are in college. Ask your school counselor about job opportunities on campus that relate to your major. Library assistants, resident assistants, teaching assistants, and computer lab assistants are all excellent opportunities for students to earn extra money on campus. You might not be eligible for some of these positions as a freshman, but if the opportunities interest you, start looking into them early. Some of these positions are highly sought after and can be competitive to land.

Off-Campus Jobs

Many college students will look off campus for job opportunities. Look in the local area for places that offer part-time employment. Some popular jobs for college students include working at a restaurant, working at a bank, working as a receptionist or office assistant at a local business, and telemarketing. Check your school's Web site, newspaper, and radio station to find out opportunities in your area. If you want to try to study while you work, ask potential employers if you will be able to do so. If you are working a desk job or answering phone calls, you might be able to catch up on some reading while you work. Restaurant jobs can offer more money in less time. Ask older students what places they recommend in your local area for students seeking part-time work.

Think creatively when it comes to earning extra money in college. You might be able to use your current skills or hobbies to earn extra cash. Babysitting might be an option for students who like children. You might even be able to babysit for some of your professors or other staff at your college. If you are interested in this option, see if you can list a babysitter-available posting in your college's newspaper. You can also post notes on your college's bulletin boards around campus to try to drum up some business. If you are computer savvy, you might be able to work tech support for a company or offer your own private tech support business. You can market your services to other students and even campus staff. If writing is your forte, you might offer editing services to other students. Try to use your skills to find a job that best suits you.

Internships

Internships offer college students valuable experience that helps students get a job after college. Some internships pay fairly well, and others pay little or no money. Check into internship opportunities in your chosen field. If gaining experience is most important to you, you might find it useful to take on an internship, even if it is unpaid. Ask your college counselor about these opportunities. If you know a company that you would like to work for after college, contact it directly about internship programs it offers. Internships will give you an advantage after you graduate college over students who have no experience. If you know your major and already know the field you want to work in when you graduate, an internship can be a solid addition to your résumé. You might even find a full-time job waiting for you after you graduate at the same place where you interned.

The Juggling Act

If you do take on a job while you are in school, you face an added challenge as compared with students who do not work. Not only will you be juggling your school and social life, you will also be trying to fit in your work schedule. Be sure to establish priorities when it comes to school, your job, and social activities. Of course, school should come first. Make sure your work schedule allows plenty of time for studying and class time. Talk to your employer about your schedule during the interview process. Tell the interviewer the number of hours you are willing to work, and be sure the job will not schedule you for more than what you request. If you find that your work schedule is taking too much time away from studying, talk to your employer about cutting back your hours.

When it comes to the priority list, your social life is on the bottom. You may have to sacrifice a night out with friends because you need to study or you are scheduled to work. Try to create a schedule you are comfortable with so that you do not feel like you are missing out. Allow one night a week or one night every couple of weeks to hang out with friends. Do not start skipping class to work or skipping study time to hang out with your friends. Your grades will suffer if your priorities are not in line. Do not take on more hours at work than you must. Bear in mind that your whole adult life after graduation will be filled with work. There is no point in overloading your work hours while you are still in school.

Other Options

Look into other options for money if you are working because you need the money for school but cannot seem to manage the schedule or you feel as if you do not have a life when you are working and going to school. There are many scholarships out there for students who are willing to look for them. Ask your financial aid office about resources to find scholarships and grants. This money will not have to be repaid, so you will not be adding to your student loans if you can find scholarships or grants available. Loans are always an option as well. You might need to look into getting loans to help out with your expenses while you are in college. Be careful not to think of this money as free money. You might be charged interest on borrowed money while you are in school, and even if your interest is waived while you are a student, the more loans you have, the more money you will owe when you graduate.

If you are interested in joining the military after you have graduated, check into your school's Reserve Officer Training Corps (ROTC) program. These programs might offer money while you are in school. The military might also offer a deal where if you commit a certain number of years of service after you graduate, the military will agree to pay off some or all of your student loans.

Case Study: Juggling School, Work, and Social Life

Alan Acosta, Residence Coordinator
University Housing, Florida State University

Juggling work, school, and a social life can be difficult for students, Alan Acosta said. The important thing is to not forget priorities. Freshmen must not forget that they are in school to get an education and must stay focused on that. Freshmen should keep their academic responsibilities in mind when they choose the job that they get and decide what kind of social life to have.

There are going to be many opportunities in college, so freshmen must choose the ones they are most interested in and feel will benefit them the most and then set their schedule accordingly.

When it comes to time management, Acosta said students should write things down. Some people live and die by their planner, and others simply fly by the seat of their pants. If freshmen write things down, they can see what they are committed to and it will help them organize their time appropriately. If they need to, freshmen should block out time to eat and study. Budgeting their time this exactly will help them be realistic about how much free time they have.

Students concerned about balancing these things should get a job on campus so they might be able to study or complete academic requirements while they work.

As for their social life, Acosta said freshmen must be sure that they are engaging in healthy socialized events. It can be incredibly easy for students to develop bad party habits. A healthy balance is necessary for students, because not engaging in a healthy social release will cause mental and emotional strain, and partying too much will almost certainly have a serious impact on grades.

Case Study: Juggling School, Work, and Social Life

Eric Booth, M.A., Director of Residence Life
Reinhardt College

Eric Booth's advice for juggling school, work, and a social life is to set priorities and remember education should be number one. If students prepare early, they will have more time to work and be social, Booth said.

Ashley Chittum, Sophomore
Tennessee Wesleyan College

Being in a sorority, working part time, being a full-time student, playing volleyball, and trying to maintain a social life made Ashley Chittum's life busy for sure. She said she keeps track of her schedule in her head but knows that keeping an organizer helps many students juggle such busy lives.

Carolynn S. Nath, Area Coordinator
University of Central Florida

Finding balance is an extremely personal thing for students, according to Carolynn Nath. She said campus offices and possibly classes can help students learn what will work for them. These may include the career center, academic advisors, academic success center, or a first-year seminar course. These classes/program sessions can help students learn different study techniques and how to study, manage time, and create a working schedule that they can tailor to their life style.

Matthew Gramling, Sophomore
Oglethorpe College

Matthew Gramling held a work-study position at his school's bookstore. He earned enough money to have spending cash for the month, had his hours of work limited by the school, and was able to complete some homework while working. He suggested that students trying to juggle school, work, and a social life not forget that school should always come first.

Frederica Anderson, Sophomore
Savannah College of Art and Design

Frederica Anderson said she knows this juggling act is possible, because she

Case Study: Juggling School, Work, and Social Life

has done it. Her advice to freshmen is to limit their hours of work, give themselves a deadline for when school assignments must be done, and plan to hang out with friends only on the weekends.

James Johns, Professional Student
Georgia Highlands College

James Johns said a student's freshman year is spent mostly on prioritizing life. Students must decide if they want to party all night and skip class, if they want to work hard, or drop out to work for a company.

Ryan Thompson, 2008 Graduate
Southern Polytechnic State University

There is no special formula, plan, or schedule to be able to juggle work, school, and a social life, Ryan Thompson said. He recommended that students try to have a healthy balance of all three to maintain sanity.

Graduation

Although this book focuses on your freshman year of college, college is four years long, at least. Depending on how many classes you schedule per semester and what your major is (and how many times your change it), college might last five years just to complete your undergraduate degree. But college is a marathon, not a sprint. Do not try to accomplish everything you want to do in college in your first year, let alone your first week. Take your time and plan ahead. Most important, stay focused on your goal: graduation.

CHAPTER 19

Three Years to Go

Although you should be proud of yourself for navigating your first year of school, your job is not over. You still have three more years to go — at least. You might need five years to complete your bachelor's degree if you plan on double-majoring. Some students are looking ahead to two more years in graduate school. But many of the tips offered in this book will help you throughout your entire college life.

Plan Ahead

Just as you scheduled out your freshman year classes before you started your first class, you should look ahead to your four years of school. Schedule your classes out for all four years while you are still a freshman. Of course, you might change your mind about your classes, and if your major changes, your schedule of classes will obviously change too. But having a schedule for all four years will help you see what classes you need to take at what time and help you more realistically manage your class schedule for your entire four years. If you do not plan ahead, you might find yourself as a senior taking freshman-level classes that you missed. Do not count on your college advisors to take care of your scheduling for you. The counselors are there to assist you, but it is your responsibility to make sure you graduate on time.

Make Goals

Set goals for each year of school. If you are thinking of studying abroad in your senior year or want to take on an internship by your junior year, write it down. For each year of college, have a list of goals that you want to accomplish during that year. Your goals might be to maintain a 3.0 GPA or better or maybe to attend at least one kegger a week. Whatever your goals are, write them down. At the beginning of each year, review the goals you set. Go back to your original mission statement for your college career and make any necessary changes. Setting goals early will help you to be more successful in the long run. Do not get too upset if you do not accomplish all your goals. Recall the saying that if you aim for the moon and fall short, you still land among the stars. So go ahead and aim high.

Words of Encouragement

Do not give up no matter how hard things seem at the time. Think back to when you were in high school and you thought the biology test was going to kill you or that you would never pass chemistry class. Somehow you made it through, and now you are in college and facing new challenges every day. Some days things will seem hard, even unbearable, but do not be discouraged. Think of how amazing it will feel to walk across that stage and get your diploma. Stay focused on the goal and keep your head up high. Consider the following words of inspiration.

Words of Encouragement

Act as if it were impossible to fail.

— Dorothea Brande

The greatest pleasure in life is doing what people say you cannot do.

— Walter Bagehot

One hundred percent of the shots you do not take do not go in.

— Wayne Gretzky

To accomplish great things we must not only act but also dream, not only plan but also believe.

— Anatole

The purpose of life is a life of purpose.

— Robert Byrne

What lies behind us and what lies before us are tiny matters to what lies within us.

— Ralph Waldo Emerson

Whether you think you can or you think you cannot, you're right.

— Henry Ford

Words of Encouragement

Procrastination is like a credit card; it is a lot of fun until you get the bill.

— Christopher Parker

How sad would be November if we had no knowledge of the Spring!

— Edwin Way Teale

If we attend continually and promptly to the little that we can do, we shall long be surprised to find out how little remains that we cannot do.

— Samuel Butler

All men who have turned out worth anything have had the chief hand in their own education.

— Sir Walter Scott

You can only keep one thought in your mind at a time, so make it a good one.

— Norman Vincent Peale

Knowledge is the frontier of tomorrow.

— Denis Waitley

Each of us is given a pocketful of time to spend however we may. We use what we will. We waste what we will. But we can never get back a day.

— Roger Wilcox

CHAPTER 20

Getting to Graduation

Imagine a fine spring day. The sun is shining brightly, a gentle breeze rustles the lush green grass under your feet. Somewhere in the distance, you hear a sweet tune as a small bird sings a song. The day seems perfect, and as you look around, you see your family and friends all watching you, all smiling proudly. Your name is called and you stand and walk slowly, majestically across the stage. You are handed your diploma, a symbol of the hard work and dedication that you have worked the last four years to get. As you pose for your picture at the end of the stage, your mind flashes back to all the good times you have been through while you were in college. You recall the friends you made, the late-night study sessions, the parties, the laughs, the smelly dorm rooms, the pink shirts from your first attempt at laundry. You think back to all of it — the times you thought you would never make it through and the times you knew you could make it. Somehow, all of it now seems worth it. All the challenges you went through seem to have added something valuable to this piece of paper you now hold in your hands. Also, you realize as you close this one door, so many more will be opening.

Your graduation day, even if it rains or you trip walking across the stage, will feel amazing. You will be proud of yourself and you will know that your family and friends are proud of you too. My own graduation was nothing like the above idealized scenario. It was held in the gym and was crammed full of hot, sweaty, and yes, smelly family, friends, and graduates. The school band played "Pomp and Circumstance" in the most out-of-tune, off-beat way imaginable. The commencement speaker, although a published author, spoke of rats and trash — not a topic any of us expected to hear at our graduation. I could not find my family in the crowd, and the announcer mispronounced my last name. Despite all that, my graduation day was one of the happiest, proudest days of my life. Looking back, I would not trade it.

As you journey through college, do not forget to stay focused on your goal. Picture your graduation day. Imagine you are chosen valedictorian. Write your speech and use it to inspire yourself when things start to get hard. When you fail a test or even a class, bear in mind that you do not have to win every leg of the race; you just have to keep going to make it to the finish line. Whatever pitfalls you might face or road blocks you come across, keep going. Do not let anything or anyone keep you from graduation.

Learning is truly a lifelong process, and your goal in college, besides graduating, should be to learn as much as possible. Learn about history, the world around you, other cultures, your own culture, yourself, relationships, laundry, driving a stick-shift car, and everything else you can learn. Be thirsty for knowledge and continually seek ways to quench that thirst. Be a positive inspiration to your friends and classmates, and help them realize the value of learning too.

Many people say their college years were the best times of their lives. As you go through your college years, you may not always believe that to be true, but do not forget that someday, you will look back and think fondly of your time in school. Take tons of pictures. Make scrapbooks of you and your friends to help recall the good times after you are out of school. Have your friends write notes about what they recall of a certain event and keep those notes in your scrapbook. Although college yearbooks may offer some memories, they will not be as personal as your own homemade scrapbook will be. Keep concert ticket stubs and receipts from special dinners, the handwritten bar-napkin note that your boyfriend wrote to you. Keep all the little things that mean something to you.

The address book that you started before you left for college should be kept and continually added to while you are in school. Keep track of all your friends. Some friends you make in your freshman year in school might not keep in touch with you even through your college years, but maybe years later, you will open that address book up and look up your first good college friend. Keep your book up to date and keep in touch with as many people as you can.

Final Words

Realistically, not every freshman who starts college will make it to graduation. As the U.S. Census Bureau reports, more than 500,000 students begin their freshman year of college each year, and so this book is needed, especially considering that the almost half of these 500,000 freshmen students will not make it to graduation, according to American Testing (ACT). ACT also reports 25 percent of freshmen will not finish their second year of college. Using the tips in this book, you should be able to stay focused on your goal to graduate and successfully survive not only your freshman year of college, but your entire college career as well.

Be proud of yourself for getting through high school and for getting to the end of this book. With any luck, you have learned some valuable skills to help you successfully survive your freshman year in school. More than that, I hope you have learned how to do well and have fun in all your years of college. Keep this book handy, share it with a friend, or use it to prop up the shortest leg on your kitchen table. Just do not forget to have fun in school, learn everything you can, and make the most of every opportunity you are given in college and in life.

Case Study: Dropouts

Alan Acosta, Residence Coordinator
University Housing, Florida State University

Alan Acosta said that there are three main reasons freshmen drop out. The first is that they are not prepared for the academic rigors of college. Many students come to college under the assumption that following their high school academic habits will bring success in college. Students do not understand that it takes much work to succeed in college and that they must be committed to putting in the effort necessary for college academic success.

The second reason is that they do not feel the emotional or mental support necessary for success in college. Acosta said that he has witnessed students who get homesick or do not feel that they belong that end up dropping out of school because the feelings were overwhelming. The third reason is that a major crisis (normally involving family) occurs, requiring the student to leave. Acosta said some students leave because a family member dies, their parents get divorced, or an older family member needs assistance. He has also seen female students leave because they get pregnant or a man and woman leave because they are getting married. Whether a freshman stays at an institution has a lot to do with where he or she is in life, whether that be academically, emotionally, or mentally, or whether the student has the maturity to handle his or her own life.

Eric Booth, M.A., Director of Residence Life
Reinhardt College

Besides dropping out due to the cost of school, according to Eric Booth, most college dropouts leave because of a lack of preparation while in high school.

Case Study: Dropouts

Booth said that with the advent of text messaging and instant messaging, students are not using proper English skills and need to focus more on proper communication.

Kelly R. Doel, Area Coordinator
University of Central Florida

Kelly Doel said that many factors can affect the success of freshmen, and students who struggle to find life balance often do not succeed. She said that the students that party too much and lose focus on their academics find it too difficult to catch up. Commonly, students allow themselves to be negatively influenced by others and engage in risky behavior, get into debt, and fail academically, Doel warned.

Ashley Chittum, Sophomore
Tennessee Wesleyan College

Ashley Chittum said students drop out of college because they are not motivated to make it to graduation. Some students, she said, would rather go straight into their career rather than go through four more years of school.

Carolynn S. Nath, Area Coordinator
University of Central Florida

The most common student dropouts that Carolynn Nath sees are the freshmen or sophomores who did not make at least a 2.0 or even 1.5 GPA for two consecutive semesters. (Each institution has a GPA requirement to meet to be classified as a student or a student on academic probation.) Working at a university and instructing courses, she sees many students create stories to get out of exams. They were too hung over from the "best night ever" or "this emergency happened," and then they fail an exam. Professors and instructors have more often than not heard the excuses and will ask for documentation supporting "_____'s death" or "_____ had to go to the hospital" or "being sick with _____." They will also follow up with these individuals or doctors to verify students' documentation. In any case, she said falsifying documents could lead to a student being held for academic dishonesty. This means a student would have to go through a conduct or honor review, which can ultimately result in

Case Study: Dropouts

documentation on transcripts, loss of scholarships or financial aid, or suspension from school. Students need to think of the consequences before creating a "little white lie" to get out of class.

On another note, although exams and presentations are an extremely large chunk of students' grades, an even larger part is attendance. She often sees students plan to take their two "free absences" on certain days around national holidays or close to winter or fall breaks. Then, an emergency occurs and the student has already used the two free absences, thus bringing his or her grade down (possibly an entire letter grade) because of missing three days of class. In a summer or short-term course, the work for one class is almost equivalent to a week's work of class, she said. So, missing class makes it difficult for a student to play catch up.

Nath advised students to organize themselves and make sure they keep track of when coursework, projects, and exams are due.

She also said that some students need to realize that a four-year institution is not for them. They want a major that is not at their university, but their community college or a specialized training center has it. Students may often feel that they let their family down by leaving school, but it is important for them to use their academic advisors so they are able to transfer credits to the new college. She said students should not feel forced to study and work in a field they are not happy in.

Matthew Gramling, Sophomore
Oglethorpe College

Matthew Gramling said he has seen freshmen transfer schools because their grades were not high enough at his school. He said some freshmen cannot handle their new freedom, party too much, and flunk out of school. Other reasons freshmen drop out are family issues or lack of money, or they do not like the school they attend.

Frederica Anderson, Sophomore
Savannah College of Art and Design

Frederica Anderson said the biggest reason freshmen drop out is because

Case Study: Dropouts

they cannot keep up with the workload and fail. They either partied too much or got so involved in a relationship that they pushed their school work aside.

James Johns, Professional Student
Georgia Highlands College

James Johns said that with students' newfound freedom, it is hard for them to resist the urge to always do what they want to do instead of what they should. He advised, "Freedom is a double-edged sword; do not let it cut you."

Ryan Thompson, 2008 Graduate
Southern Polytechnic State University

The biggest reason most college freshmen drop out of school is due to not knowing how to balance things in their lives such as work, family, and a personal life. Ryan Thompson said students make the mistake of not arranging things in their life around school, rather than having their school responsibilities come first. Because they are freshmen and have a choice to go to classes, they choose not to. Some students, Thompson said, just need someone to tell them to go to class.

Checklists, Questionnaires, and More

Monthly Budgeting Worksheet			
Income		**Expenses**	
Your pay	$	Rent	$
Money from parents	$	Utilities (gas, electric, and water)	$
Tips	$	Cable, Internet, landline	$
Other income	$	Insurance (home, auto, life, and health)	$
	$	Food (eating out, ordering in, groceries, snacks, and school food plan)	$
	$	School supplies (pens, paper, and notebooks)	$
	$	Clothing	$
	$	Auto (gas and maintenance)	$
	$	Cell phone	$
	$	Health (medical, dental, and over-the-counter medications)	$
	$	Entertainment (movies, concerts, and music downloads)	$
	$	Gifts (holidays and birthdays)	$

Monthly Budgeting Worksheet			
Income		**Expenses**	
	$	Household (shampoo, cleaning supplies, etc.)	$
	$	Savings account (try to save 10 percent of income)	$
	$	Emergency fund/ incidentals	$
	$	Other expenses	$
Totals	$	Totals	$

Roommate Questionnaire

1. Are you a night owl or an early bird?

2. Do you have siblings?

3. Are you the oldest/youngest/middle child?

4. Do you have pets at home?

5. What type of music do you listen to?

6. What ground rules do you want to establish? Do you want to have a roommate agreement or constitution? (Some colleges provide samples of these where roommates can fill in certain rules about visitations and quiet hours.)

7. Do you snore? Are you a heavy or light sleeper?

8. What are you bringing for the dorm room? What do I need to bring? (Think about televisions, microwave, fridge, coffee maker, and computer.)

9. Do you like to party, or are you more of a homebody?

10. Are you shy or outgoing?

11. Do you have a car that you are bringing to school?

12. How close is your hometown to school? Will you be staying at school over the weekends?

13. What is your religious background? Are you open-minded to other points of view?

14. Is your hometown a small community or big city?

15. What are your hobbies?

16. Do you play sports, and if so, what sports?

17. Do you play a musical instrument? Will you be practicing in the dorm room?

18. What is your favorite food, movie, book, and color?

19. What are your political viewpoints?

20. Do you smoke cigarettes?

21. Do you plan on joining a sorority/fraternity or other clubs/ organizations?

22. What is your major? What classes are you taking first semester?

23. What are your study habits (study in total quiet or with music)?

24. Are you clean or messy? (Discuss dividing up chores/cleaning the dorm and your roommates' expectations for the room condition.)

25. What are your pet peeves?

26. Are you hot- or cold-natured? (Discuss room temperature.)

And just for kicks …

27. Have you ever tried to build a time machine out of a DeLorean?

28. Do you have an obsession with any particular soft drink brand?

COURSE SCHEDULE WORKSHEET				
Rank of Class (1-10)	Name of Class	Times Offered	Pre-requisites	Seasonal

Packing Checklist
Computer
Flip-flops and shower bag
Clothes, including shoes and outerwear
Clothes hamper, laundry soap, and supplies
Storage bins
Music, stereo, guitar
A touch of home
First-aid kit
Alarm clock
Backpack, school supplies
Cell phone and charger or calling card
Day planner or organizer
Address book or list
Bedding and pillow(s)
Cleaning supplies (broom, sponge, or scrub brush for washing dishes, dish soap, and all-purpose cleaners, for example)
Dishes
Board games and cards
Appliances that are allowed (microwave, coffee maker, toaster, hot plate, George Foreman grill, and iron)
Desk lamp
Dry-erase and/or bulletin boards
Sewing kit
TV and DVD player
Bicycle
Journal
Emergency car kit
Vacuum (check to see if you can check one out for your dorm before you bring one)
College registration forms

Experts' Biographies

Frederica Anderson

Sophomore

Savannah College of Art and Design

Frederica Anderson was born in Baltimore, Maryland, on September 30, 1988, where she lived until August 1999. She moved to Columbus, Georgia, where she attended middle school and high school. She was a part of the Justice and Military Professional Academy and graduated as number 13 in her class. She is a Performing Arts major at Savannah College of Art and Design (SCAD) with a minor in dance. She has appeared in numerous student films and also has done voice-over work for sound design students attending SCAD. She is also a member of the Black Student Association. Her future plans include becoming a member of the SCAD Ensemble, completing her undergraduate degree, and pursuing a master's degree in performing arts and dance.

Alan Acosta

Residence Coordinator

University Housing

Florida State University

Alan Acosta

942 Learning Way

P.O. Box 3064174

Tallahassee, FL 32313-4174

Phone: (850) 644-3558

Fax: (850) 645-7751

E-mail: aacosta@admin.fsu.edu

Alan Acosta began in housing as an RA at the University of Florida (UF), where he worked from 2001 to 2004. After completing his bachelor of science in business administration (BSBA) degree in business management, he stayed at UF and worked as a graduate hall director from 2004 to 2006 while completing his master's degree in education with a concentration in student personnel in higher education. During the summer of 2005, he worked as an Association of College and University Housing Officers-International (ACUHO-I) intern at The New School, a university in New York City. He has worked as a Residence Coordinator at Florida State University since July 2006.

Eric Booth

M.A., former Director of Residence Life

Reinhardt College

P.O. Box 853

Waleska, GA 30183

Eric Booth arrived at Reinhardt College in July 2006 after spending three years in residence life at Texas Lutheran University (Seguin, Texas) and two years at Waldorf College (Forest City, Iowa). While working at Texas Lutheran, he obtained his master's degree in

Eric Booth

higher education administration from the University of Texas at San Antonio. He earned a bachelor's degree from William Penn University.

Kelly R. Doel

Area Coordinator

University of Central Florida

kdoel@mail.ucf.edu

Kelly Doel has been an area coordinator with the department of housing and residence life at the University of Central Florida for three years. Kelly began her career at Florida Atlantic University after attending the University of Florida (UF), where she earned degrees in English and secondary English education. While attending UF, she worked as an RA and graduate hall director for the department of housing and residence education.

James Johns

Georgia Highlands College

Born in Rome, Georgia, **James Johns** grew up 15 miles away in Cartersville. He graduated from Cartersville High in 2001. In his senior year of high school, he was able to start college, so his first year in college was in the fall of 2000. He attended Floyd (Highlands) College for one year and then transferred to Kennesaw State for one year. He decided to take a semester off from school to work and then moved to Honolulu, Hawaii. There he attended Kapi'olani Community College (KCC) from the fall of 2003 to the fall of 2006. He graduated with an associate's degree in liberal arts. In the fall of 2005, he was accepted into the nursing program at KCC but decided to study Japanese and live in Japan. From fall 2005 to summer 2006, Johns studied Japanese and spent the last

James Johns

three months in Kanagawa, Japan. He attended Tokai University, where he was active in an international relations group and an avid traveler. In December of 2006, he moved back to Georgia to be with his family and to finish school. He is currently a student a Georgia Highlands College in Rome, Georgia, where he is waiting to start nursing school again.

Derek Linn

University of Arkansas

Derek Linn is a junior at the University of Arkansas studying landscape architecture. He enjoys playing, writing, and listening to music. He likes the town of Fayetteville, Arkansas, where his school is located, and enjoys exploring the Arkansas Ozarks when time allows.

Carolynn S. Nath

University of Central Florida

Area Coordinator

Department of Housing and Residence Life

Carolynn S. Nath received her bachelor of arts degree from the University of South Florida, master of science degree from Indiana University-Bloomington, and is working on her master's in business administration at the University of Central Florida. She has work experience with collegiate offices in on-campus, off-campus, and affiliated student housing. She also has worked with student conduct and academic dishonesty review boards and has additional experience with athletics and alumni associations and as a faculty member. Nath has researched and presented at regional and national conferences on the following topics:

Carolynn S. Nath

social justice issues, safety and security, diversity education, sustainability and the collegiate environment, communication, and program and leadership development, along with other issues facing institutions of higher education for both students and staff. She is actively involved with the following national organizations: American College Personnel Association, National Association of Student Personnel Administrators, Association for Student Judicial Affairs, and the Association for College and University Housing Officers-International.

Ryan Thompson

Southern Polytechnic State University

Resources

52 Ways to Get Along With Your College Roommate

Catherine E. Rollins

Publisher: Thomas Nelson; (June 1994)

Roommates, College Sublets, and Living in the Dorm

Patrique

Publisher: Scojtia Pub Co; (December 1989)

College Life 101: The Roommate

Wendy Corsi Staub

Publisher: Berkeley Publishing Group

Helpful Web sites

www.collegeview.com offers helpful advice and tips to college-bound students.

www.students-4-students.com offers advice for students by students.

www.iamnext.com/academics offers articles and tips to help the college student with common issues that may arise.

www.clarkhoward.com: Consumer advocate and financial guru Clark Howard offers excellent tips on budgeting, retirement savings, purchasing cars and houses, and cheap travel deals.

www.sparknotes.com is like an online version of CliffNotes. It might be a helpful reference to understanding a book that you would not otherwise understand, but do not rely too heavily on it. Many professors know what SparkNotes says about a literary work and will be able to tell if you read the book or just read the SparkNotes.

www.collegehumor.com: A Web site just for fun.

Amazon.com: For all your shopping needs. Search for cheaper textbooks, gifts for family members, or just about anything.

www.barnesandnoble.com: Check prices on textbooks or other required reading materials. After you sign up, watch your inbox for e-mail coupons toward future purchases.

www.half.ebay.com: Check for new and used textbooks on this eBay-related site.

www.classmates.com: If you lost touch with a high school classmate, you can search for him or her on this Web site. This service requires a subscription in order to contact people.

www.myspace.com: Create your own Web site to share pictures and blogs with friends. Also try Facebook.

www.facebook.com: Similar to MySpace, create your own site to share your experiences with friends and family online.

www.studentuniverse.com: If you are thinking of traveling to Europe, this site offers excellent resources. You can also search for cheaper domestic and international flights on this site.

www.tripadvisor.com: Get travel advice, from finding a good price on airfare to getting the real scoop on a specific hotel or travel package.

www.eloan.com: Financial information can be found on this site. You can also get your credit rating free on this site.

www.bankrate.com: Compare credit cards and get other helpful financial information on this site.

www.ratemyprofessors.com: Before you sign up for classes, check out this Web site. Students use this site to post information on professors. Find out what other students think about professors before you sign up for a class. If you go to a small school or the professor you are searching for is new, you might not find information on this site.

www.Evite.com: If you want to throw a party or just plan a pizza night with friends, **Evite.com** can help you design an online invitation to e-mail to your friends. It provides an easy way to keep track of how many people are attending your function and makes it easy to e-mail out additional information to those who have responded yes to the invitation.

www.monster.com: Search for job listings in your area or nationwide with this Web site. You can also find helpful information about writing your résumé and cover letter, salary ranges for specific fields, and interviewing tips.

www.careerbuilder.com: Search similar topics to **Monster.com**'s Web site. It is good to compare the information of both of these sites to get the most accurate information possible.

www.collegeboard.com: For broad advice on surviving college, check out this site. You will also find information on writing shorthand, which will come in handy when you are frantically trying to take notes in class.

www.niaaa.nih.gov: This site offers information on alcoholism and sources for help if you or someone you know might be suffering from this disease.

www.mypyramid.gov: If you do not recall the food pyramid, check it out here. Other nutrition tips can also be found on this site.

www.bbbs.org: If you are interested in volunteer opportunities, this site features Big Brother and Big Sisters.

Glossary of College Terms

Academic probation: This program identifies students with cumulative grade point averages below 2.0, or a C.

Academic year: An academic year consists of the fall and spring semesters, plus the summer session.

Accreditation: Your college/university is certified by an organization or organizations to ensure quality standards are being met for the institution as well as for specific degree programs. A list of accrediting agencies can be found at **www.ed.gov**.

Admission: Your college admission is when you accept a school's offer of enrollment.

Advisor: Advisors are counselors, professors, or other faculty members who offer advice on academics and class scheduling to students.

Associate degree: Often two-year programs, associate degrees are awarded after completing about 60 semester units in a specific field of study.

Audit: Many schools offer auditing, which allows you to take a class or classes without receiving a grade or credit for the class. After you enroll in a course for credit, most schools will not allow you to change the status to audit. Check your school's audit policy for more information.

Bachelor's degree: This degree is commonly completed in four years and is awarded after you complete 120 to 124 semester hours of coursework in a certain field of study or academic program.

Catalog: Your school's catalog will contain information including degree program requirements, course descriptions and prerequisites, school policies, academic calendar, faculty names, and important phone numbers.

Certificate: Certificates verify that a student has completed a certain course or courses in a field of study.

Class schedule: Your school's class schedule might be available online, in a paper format, or both. The schedule will list the name of the course, course number, times and dates the classes are being offered, the location, and the professor teaching the course.

Core requirements: Core requirements refer to courses that are mandatory for all students to take to graduate from the college with a specified major.

Course numbers: Each course will have a specific number assigned to it that may contain a few letters designating the area of study and numbers designating the level of the course. For example, ENG365 might be a junior level literature class.

Courses: Classes in college may be referred to as courses. All the available courses that your college offers will be listed in the school's catalog. Some courses might not be offered every semester, and some may be offered only once per year. Planning your class schedule ahead of time will help make sure you do not miss out on courses that are not offered every semester.

Credit hour: Each college course is worth a set number of credit hours, and you need a specific number of credit hours to graduate. Each school is different. Check your student course catalog, student handbook, or meet with your advisor to find out exactly what you need.

Curriculum (program): A curriculum or program is the list of your school's requirements for courses, internships, or theses to graduate with a degree in that area.

Cut: Cutting class is when you miss a class session without prior approval from your professor or for an unapproved reason.

Degree plan: This term is similar to the curriculum or program. A degree plan outlines the course requirements for a student to graduate with a specific degree.

Departments: Your school will be separated into different departments for academics (by degree programs) and by services (financial aid, admissions).

Distance learning: Common today, distance learning classes are often held online, but any class not held within a traditional classroom setting is considered distance learning. Some of these courses will be self-paced, and other times professors will lead the courses and require students to post homework assignments weekly.

Doctoral degree: This degree is the most advanced you can earn. A doctoral degree takes eight years or more to complete.

Drop and add: After you have enrolled in classes for the semester, there will be a time period allotted by your school to make changes to your schedule. Check your school's policy on drop/add before you make changes so that you are not charged for a course unnecessarily or receive a failing grade in a class you thought you dropped but were not able to drop.

Elective: Any course that is not a requirement in your specific degree plan or curriculum is considered an elective. Students can choose these courses, although the program might stipulate that electives must be within certain fields of study. For example, for an English degree, your school might require a certain number of English department electives.

FAFSA: The Free Application for Federal Student Aid is a form that can be filled out annually by current and anticipating university students (both undergraduate and graduate), and sometimes their parents, to determine their eligibility for federal student financial aid. Find the form at **www.fafsa.ed.gov**.

Fees: Any costs related to your enrollment in college are considered fees. These fees include tuition and academic expenses as well as student activity fees.

Financial aid: Any monetary assistance you receive for being enrolled in college is considered financial aid. Types of aid include scholarships, work-study jobs, loans, and grants.

Flat-rate tuition: Some colleges have started charging all full-time students a flat rate of tuition regardless of how many semester hours they are taking above 12 hours.

Freshman: Any student with fewer than 30 hours of college credit completed. This number may vary at each school and whether your school is on semesters or quarters. Check with your advisor to be sure of your classification.

Full-time student: Students enrolled in 12 or more credit hours per semester are considered full-time students.

GED (General Education Development examination): This examination shows equivalency to a high school diploma for students who did not graduate from high school.

General Education requirement (Gen-eds): Gen-eds are courses required for all students who are graduating from a college or university.

GPA: Your grade point average or GPA is the average of your class grades and is based on a 4.0 scale, similar to your high school's calculation.

Grants: Grants are a type of financial assistance that do not require repayment.

GRE (Graduate Record Examination): A standardized, multiple-choice test for admission into graduate school given by the Educational Testing Service. Colleges use these test scores to make admissions decisions. It is similar to the SAT, only it is for admission to a graduate program instead of to an undergraduate program.

Half-time student: Students enrolled in six credit hours per semester are considered half-time students.

Internship: Some schools require students to take a job in their specific field of study before they can earn a degree in that area. Some students elect to complete an internship even if it is not required for their degree program. Internships can be paid, unpaid, or stipend-based compensation.

Junior: Any student with 60 to 89 college credit hours completed is considered a junior. This number may vary at each school and whether your school is on semesters or quarters. Check with your advisor to be sure of your classification.

Loans: Loans are a type of financial assistance that must be repaid.

Some loans do not require repayment until after a student is out of school, and others require immediate payments.

Major: A major is a field of study that students select to focus on a specific field of study or area of concentration.

Master's degree: After completing a bachelor's degree, students might desire a more advanced degree in a similar or different area than they focused on for their undergraduate degree. An additional two years of college is required to complete this graduate-level degree program.

Minor: Students might select an area to focus on other than their major. Students can minor in another field of study by completing some courses in that field without having to complete as many courses as would be required to major in that field.

Nonresident: Most colleges charge different tuition rates for residents and nonresidents within their state. Students who are nonresidents live in another state when not enrolled in school or have not lived in the same state their college is in for at least a year. Schools might have differing residency requirements, and so be sure to check with your school on how they deem residents versus nonresidents.

Online courses: Courses or classes that are offered online or through the Internet.

Part-time student: Any student taking fewer than 12 credit hours in a semester is considered part time.

Prerequisite: Some courses have requirements before students can enroll in the class. A prerequisite is the course that has to be completed (with a minimum grade) before another class can be taken.

Private university: A private college or university does not receive state assistance, which means it gets funding from private sources, tuition, and fees.

Professor: Refer to the breakdown of professor types in Chapter 6. The general term can refer to any faculty member or teaching staff.

Provost: Many colleges use this title for senior academic administrators although the actual job duties of a provost may be different at various schools.

Public university: Colleges or universities that receive state assistance are considered public schools.

Registration: During the registration time period each semester, students must enroll in the next semester's classes.

Resident: A student who lives in the same state as the school or meets his or her school's residency requirements is considered a resident and may receive a cheaper tuition than nonresidents.

Resident Assistant (RA): A student leader who supervises students living in a residence hall or dorm and lives in the same dorm. These students receive cheaper or free room and board.

Rolling admission: When you apply to schools, find out if they have a rolling admission program. If so, apply as early as possible. A school with rolling admission will accept students as they apply and does not wait until all applications are received before they begin sending out acceptance letters.

Scholarships: A scholarship offers students financial assistance based on merit, whether academically based or based on other eligibility and does not require repayment.

Senior: A student with 90 or more hours of college credit completed but who has not received a bachelor's degree is a senior. In college, the years you are in school do not determine your "title." A senior might be in his or her sixth or seventh year of college. This number may vary at each school and whether your school is on semesters or quarters. Check with your advisor to be sure of your classification.

Sophomore: A sophomore is a student with 30 to 59 college credit hours completed. This number may vary at each school and whether your school is on semesters or quarters. Check with your advisor to be sure of your classification.

Stafford Loan: A Stafford Loan is a student loan offered to eligible students based on the student's FAFSA. No payments are required while the student is enrolled in school (students must be enrolled at least half-time). The repayment deferral continues for six months after the student leaves school either by graduating, dropping below half-time enrollment, or withdrawing.

Subsidized loan: With subsidized loans, the borrower is not charged interest. For this type of loan, the U.S. Department of Education pays the interest while the student is in school.

Summer session: Often six weeks long, summer sessions take place between the spring and fall semesters.

Syllabus: Professors distribute a written description of the course requirements to students at the beginning of each course. Major assignments' due dates and dates of midterms and finals are listed on the syllabus.

Teaching Assistant (TA): TAs are on a temporary assignment or contract with the college or university and are responsible for tutoring, holding office hours, grading homework or exams, leading discussion sessions, or teaching classes.

Transcript: Your transcript is the official documentation of all the courses you have taken with a college, the grade you received for the courses and the credit hours awarded for each course. Your GPA should also be included on your transcript.

Tuition: Tuition is the cost of courses you enroll in and does not include other fees associated with your general enrollment in college.

Two-for-one: Some believe in the principle that every one hour of class time should require two hours of out-of-classroom study time by the student.

Unsubsidized Loan: Unlike subsidized loans, students are charged interest during the time they are in school. Repayment is still deferred until six months after the student leaves school.

Web/online registration: Many colleges offer Web or online registration so that students can enroll in classes from any computer with Internet access.

Work-study program: Work-study programs are considered federal financial aid. Students work on campus for a set amount of money and are limited in the number of hours they can work each week.

Bibliography

Books

Anyonge, William and Mumbi Thairu. *A Survival Guide for the College Freshman: Achieving Academic Excellence.* Morris Publishing, Kearney, 2005.

Bernstein, Mark and Yadin Kaufmann, editors. *How to Survive Your Freshman Year, 2nd ed.* Hundreds of Heads Books, Atlanta, 2007.

Dickson, Deljah S. *Freshman 101: A Road Map & Journal to Surviving Your First Year of College.* PJ's Publishing, Inglewood, 2004.

Hanson, Jennifer and Friends. *The Real Freshman Handbook: A Totally Honest Guide to Life on Campus.* Houghton Mifflin Company, Boston, New York, 2002.

Malone, Michael S. *The Everything College Survival Book, 2nd ed.* Adams Media, Avon, 2005.

Students Helping Students. *Navigating Your Freshman Year: How to Make the Leap to College Life — and Land on Your Feet.* Prentice Hall Press, New York, 2005.

Turner, Matthew Paul. *Everything You Need to Know Before College*. Think, Colorado Springs, 2006.

Web sites

University of North Texas. *Glossary of College Terms*. **www.unt.edu/pais/howtochoose/glossary.htm**

Taft College. *Glossary of College Terms*. **www.taftcollege.edu/newTC/Community/glossary.htm**

Bethune-Cookman University. *Roommate Questionnaire*. **www.cookman.edu/subpages/roommate_quest.asp**

Roanoke College. *College Life 101: The Roommate*. **http://web.roanoke.edu/x3645.xml?refurl=x3645.xml**

FinAid. Student Loans. **http://www.finaid.org/loans**

Author Biography

Jessica Linnell is a freelance writer and editor living in the metro Atlanta area with her three-year-old lab mix, Monte. She earned a bachelor's degree in communications from Reinhardt College in Waleska, Georgia. Her previous works have been published in *Atlanta Magazine*, *Cherokee Living*, and other local and international trade publications. In addition to her research and writing on education, Jessica has worked for newspapers, magazines, and corporations as a writer and editor. She served ten years as a Public Health Technician with the Air Force both as active duty and in the National Guard. When she is not writing or editing, she keeps busy with hiking, backpacking, skydiving, and other adventures.

Index